T0086379

On the Tour

More City Walks

Thomas Porky McDonald

authorHOUSE®

AuthorHouse™
1663 Liberty Drive
Bloomington, IN 47403
www.authorhouse.com
Phone: 1 (800) 839-8640

Published by AuthorHouse 09/23/2017

ISBN: 978-1-5462-0722-1 (sc)
ISBN: 978-1-5462-0723-8 (e)

Print information available on the last page.

This book is printed on acid-free paper.

Other books by Thomas Porky McDonald:

An Irishman's Tribute to the Negro Leagues

Over the Shoulder and Plant on One:
An Irishman's Tribute to Willie Mays

Where the Angels Bow to the Grass: A Boy's Memoir

The Air That September

Hit Sign, Win Suit: An Irishman's Tribute to Ebbets Field

Series Endings: A Whimsical Look at the Final Plays
of Baseball's Fall Classic, 1903-2003

At a Loss to Eternity:
Baseball Teams of Note That Didn't Win it All

Never These Men: One Man's Look at Baseball's
Creatively Cultured Characters

Does the Toy Cannon Fire Still at Night?

the skipper's scrapbook

Poet in the Grandstand: An Enlightened Tour of Ballparks
and the Places Where They Live: 1990-2010

A Walk in the City: An Incomplete Tour

Poetry Collections

Ground Pork: Poems 1989-1994
Downtown Revival: Poems 1994-1997
Closer to Rona: Poems 1997-1999
Diamond Reflections: Baseball Pieces For Real Fans
Dem Poems: The Brooklyn Collection
Still Chuckin': Poems 1999-2002
In the Cameo Shade: Poems 2002-2005
Vespers at Sunset: Poems 2005-2007
And These Thy Gifts: Poems 2007-2009

Short Stories

Paradise Oval...and other Tallman Tales

Jacket Design and Formatting
by Lance Tallman

Cover Consultant, Olga Khrapovitski

Front Cover, Back Cover & photos at the
center of the book by Lance Tallman

Edited by Paula Alleyne, Asya Muid,
Olga Khrapovitski & Lisa Schwartz

This Book
is Dedicated to
all those in search
of meaning,
who celebrate it,
whenever and wherever
they find it,
then share it with
as many people
as they can.

AND TO:

All of my dear friends at
New York City Transit
1985-2016
(Lawrence, Chapel, Livingston & Broadway)
May you find safe passage home

In Memoriam

Diane Armstrong
Ravi Chinnasamy
Laverne Edwards
Ken Levy
Doris Overton
Janice Rice

Friends who shared the Transit tour with me

Are the Streets Still Running With Me?

Down about the lonely avenue,
do I wade in urchins deep?
Sometimes I wonder in the moonlight
if they trail me as I sleep.

Are the streets still running with me?
Do the shadows call my name?
Is the water bill still shifting,
in a rush, or for to claim?

Is the bus on 59th Street
just like the one I knew before?
In the event I slip in silence,
will I be hoisted from the floor?

I find the traffic in the City,
it always flows from my each whim;
Whether the lights are high and glowing,
or in a mind swept, roaring dim.

Are the streets still running with me?
Well if they are, well let it be;
I can't explain the sidewalk silhouettes,
or why they still appeal to me.

On the Tour

You're only so blessed
as where you have been;
You're only so open inside;
Through times of excess
or lives without sin,
just sit back and enjoy the ride.

Alone's not a place
for someone quite dear;
Together is where we all roam;
Should you take the pace
from those you revere,
you'll surely arrive safe at home.

Accept what you are
and thrill through the night;
So sure there is nothing for sure;
But do raise the bar
and reach for the light,
retaining all stops on the tour.

Contents

Re-Introduction

On "Actualities"

This book is a sequel to a previous offering called *A Walk in the City*, which I am guessing you might be familiar with if you are reading this now. So I won't be all that wordy getting into what is essentially a re-introduction of what the first volume was and this one is.

About four and a half years ago, I was asked to write some short pieces about baseball in New York City, or more pointedly, *City* baseball venues and how to get to them. This request was made by Lisa Schwartz, who worked for New York City Transit Corporate Communications, which put out an internal web page each day for NYC Transit called *MTA Today*. Those stories were usually about policies and other Transit-related items, but on some days, usually Fridays, Lisa and the other good folks that she worked for, Gene Ribeiro and Connie DePalma, thought to lighten things up with travel and leisure pieces for the workers. In the Summer of 2012, a complete baseball series was proposed and through friends in my department, Technology & Information Systems (TIS), three ladies who worked on the Transit website and therefore interacted regularly with Lisa and company, my name came up. So thanks again to Lisa, Gene and Connie, as well as web designers Paula Alleyne, Olga Khrapovitski and Asya Muid, three of the best friends that I made in my 31 years at Transit.

After submitting four baseball pieces – on Citi Field, the New Yankee Stadium and Macombs Dam Park, the Brooklyn Cyclones at Coney Island and a remembrance of Shea Stadium and the New York World's Fair of 1964-65 – Lisa asked if I could do an article on the then new 9/11 Memorial. That was fine with me and after visiting the

Memorial with Paula, Olga and Asya, I pumped that one out pretty quickly, too. By then, Corporate Communications had taken a liking to me and my writing, so I just kept on submitting travel pieces to them. Within a couple of years, the result would be *A Walk in the City*, which contained 65 of my vignettes and 5 profiles of books of mine which they were kind enough to slip onto the *MTA Today* page on occasion.

The first book contained many museums and places of interest that I started re-visiting or going to for the first time. They included world famous sites, as well as some places hardly known at all. In short, it was what those who live in New York think about, but don't all do, that is, see as many of the plethora of interesting and historical places in *The City* that we can. I enjoyed those days so much that the idea for a book came up. I subtitled *A Walk in the City "An Incomplete Tour,"* since there would always be more spots in New York City to go to after I was done. But I had gotten so enamored with the format of these pieces and the folks at Corporate Communications were still looking for articles to use on Fridays, so I kept on going. The result is this book, which is another, expanded collection of New York City travel pieces.

This time around, I went to a number of historic houses, after having enjoyed visiting the Merchants House Museum and the Morris-Jumel Mansion for the first book. Having gone to most of the big museums previously, I've tried to find many more niche museums that I missed the first time around and I made a concerted effort to hit the zoos, having only gone to the Central Park Zoo for *A Walk in the City.* Throw in some *City* parks, disparate theatres and miscellaneous points of interest and what you have is *On the Tour: More City Walks.*

This book was written with the same parameters that the first one had. Each piece would be around 450 words, with the final paragraph dedicated to relaying how to get to each site by train and/or bus. I have again replaced my byline from the original *MTA Today* releases with a relevant website for each piece and I've added a *Walking Distance* section at the end of each article, to highlight points of interest in the immediate area. This time around, though, I have excluded the dates that each piece appeared on *MTA Today*, due to the fact that I retired from NYC Transit about 1/3 of the way through the writing of the book and thus lost access to exactly when these internally released pieces would be used. Again, these pieces are just a guide, things I liked about each venue and my way of listing a horde of New York destinations, with the intention of being a catalyst to the reader's imagination. I don't get into details, such as the days and times when the places I go to are open or closed or the prices of any particular site. I just highlight what stuck out to me as a New Yorker, which often includes a history of the site. As such, the websites listed are essential, especially for the historic houses, which have very defined and sometimes limited visiting hours.

Back in the early 20th Century, when the Edison Company put out the very first moving pictures, they consisted of many shots of traffic in *The City*, which today would seem mundane. Back then, though, the first people ever to experience moving pictures saw something different. Edison called the clips "*Actualities*," and they were received, as you might imagine, with fascination. These two books of mine are my "*Actualities*," and though fascination is not what I expect from the audience, I do think that these volumes can be a great entry-level guide to roaming around *The City*. I have received a number of thank you messages and calls from people who have used *A Walk in the City* as a way to experience New York, or at least a part of it, so I feel confident this will be the case for *On the Tour*.

One more thing: This will be my final book on this subject. Combining both books could keep one busy for a while, if exploring New York City is your goal. The pieces in their entirety are obviously very arbitrary, just places that I thought would be fun to see and share with others. You can find plenty of tour guides that have many more destinations, which give you much more information, containing every single iota of minutia about a particular site. But if you want to use your own compass, these short vignettes, along with the websites included, will more than satisfy your curiosities, without stuffing your head with gratuitous and in my opinion, superfluous information. As I write this re-introduction, the book is about 60% complete, and I have around 35 more sites that I am considering picking from to finish it off, though I have no idea which ones will make the final cut. That's the beauty of it all, that even I don't know what I will ultimately use, until the book is done. Similarly, until the reader pages through it, he or she will not know which ones sound like places that they would like to see. Going forward, the best part might be that new, inspiring venues seem to show up on a regular basis in New York City. For instance, as this book goes to the publisher, the Jackie Robinson Museum in Lower Manhattan is set to begin construction and should be open in a few years. So hit *The City,* kiddies and if you manage to see all that I have included in *A Walk in the City* and *On the Tour*, by all means, keep looking. I know I will.

T.P. McDonald
Astoria, Queens
9/28/16

<u>Note</u>: Although I organized the book into two sections: 1) Parks, Zoos, Theatres & Other Sites and 2) Museums & Historic Houses, there were a few hybrids. Since they were right next to each other, I felt that the Prospect Park Zoo and the Lefferts Historic House Museum should be an entry, one which I decided to put in Section One. In addition, the Poe Cottage & Park, the King Manor, the Downtown Brooklyn Baseball Landmarks and the Old Stone House in Washington Park all included elements of both sections, but I opted to put them in Section Two, simply because the historic house aspect is the main impetus for visiting these venues. Walk on.

(1)

Parks, Zoos, Theatres & Other Sites

Amy's Bread

http://www.amysbread.com

New York is replete with many wonderful local bakeries, as well as different successful chains. Living in Queens all my life and working out of Brooklyn for 20 years, I have been exposed to numerous, fabulous bread and pastry shops. But the best New York City bakery I've seen in recent times is *Amy's Bread*, which has been serving some of the finest, fresh baked products in *The City* for over two decades.

In 1992, Minneapolis native Amy Scherber opened her first shop in Hell's Kitchen. She had graduated from the New York Restaurant School and had worked in three bakeries in France, before the passion to bake bread brought her back to *The City.* The first *Amy's Bread* shop was manned by only 5 employees and became, in short order, a very popular neighborhood shop. As time moved on, word of mouth grew about this endearing little place that served delicious breads and pastries. Today, with other *Amy's Bread* shops opening in places like the Cheslea Market and Bleecker Street in *The Village*, Amy's staff is close to 200 workers, though the flagship shop on 46th Street and 9th Avenue remains at the heart of the franchise.

An intangible aspect of *Amy's Bread*, spelled out on the shop's website, comes across whenever you go there. *Amy's Mission Statement* includes items like respecting the craft of traditional baking, being a good neighbor, staying local and providing service that makes you smile. Essentially, *Amy's Bread* is an old style mom-and-pop type store whose clientele has become far-reaching enough to make any bloodless chain envious.

Amy has received many awards and her business has been featured in numerous periodicals. Her Irish soda bread is a must if you are a New Yorker and the long lines outside of the shop in the days preceding the St. Patrick's Day Parade are akin to the down the block slice of humanity seen at Junior's in Brooklyn for desserts on the day before Thanksgiving. In August of 2015, *Amy's* opened a satellite shop called *The Pantry* right next door to the original, which serves handcrafted products made in Brooklyn, Upstate New York and New England. Amy's workers are pleasant and apparently treated well; on the store's 24th anniversary in 2016, they shared free pieces of cake with customers who happened by. *Amy's Bread* is one of the friendliest places in New York City.

To get to the original *Amy's Bread* in Hell's Kitchen, take the 1 to 50th Street, or the N, Q, R or W to 49th Street and walk up to the shop on 672 Ninth Avenue. The M11 bus runs on 9th Avenue to 46th Street. Check the *Amy's Bread* website for directions to the other locations.

Walking Distance: B.B. King's; Madame Tussaud's Wax Museum; Ripley's Believe It or Not Odditorium; New Victory Theater; Port Authority Bus Terminal; Hard Rock Café, New York; Intrepid Sea, Air & Space Museum; Circle Line; Signature Theatre Company; Broadway Theater District; The Meatball Shop; The Town Hall; Bryant Park; New York Public Library; Grand Central Terminal; Gulliver's Gate.

Astoria Park

www.nycgovparks.org/parks/astoria-park/

One of the great *City* parks lies on the banks of the East River, in Astoria. Situated between the overlooking Triboro and Hell Gate bridges, *Astoria Park* is a wonderful place to take a break, hang out by the shoreline or participate in a number of activities that sprinkle throughout the park. Bordered by Shore Boulevard, Ditmars Boulevard, 21st Street and Astoria Park South (which leads into Hoyt Avenue), *Astoria Park* is in a large rectangular plot, just off a residential area to the North and East and a series of factories which lead toward the 59th Street Bridge to the South.

Along the just under 60-acre landscape, there are tennis courts, a pair of children's playgrounds, bocce courts, a running track and a skate park, most of which are located in the southern part of the park. The current track replaces a former running track which used to circle around a pair of baseball fields, which all went by the wayside in the past few decades. The most significant venue within *Astoria Park* is a 54,450-square-foot pool located at the center of the park.

Astoria Pool is the oldest and largest swimming pool in New York City. It was built in 1934-36 and was used for the Olympic trials and/or qualifying events for both the 1936 and the 1964 Summer Olympics. Consisting of a main swimming pool, a wading pool and a diving pool, *Astoria Pool* has opened its waters for generations of Astoria natives. Though I have never been a swimmer, I had many friends who frequented it often. One of my very best friends, Frank Brady, swore by *Astoria Pool*, so much so that his daughter Jessica, who was taught to swim at *Astoria Pool* by her dad, became a long time lifeguard there. If you are a swimmer and live in New York, you really should make the trek to *Astoria Park* and take some laps at the legendary *Astoria Pool*, which was given New York City Landmark status on June 20, 2006.

Of the many wonderful parks in New York City, *Astoria Park* naturally holds a special place for someone like me, who has lived in Astoria his entire life. And even though the ballfields I played on as a child are no longer part of the park, a day walking through it, standing by the shore or checking out the World War I Memorial at the center of the park is well worth anyone's time.

A 10-minute walk from the N or Q train stops at either the Astoria Boulevard or Astoria-Ditmars stops brings you to *Astoria Park.* The stops on the Q69 bus from Hoyt Avenue to Ditmars along 21st Street leave you a block from *Astoria Park.*

Walking Distance: Riccardo's by The Bridge; Triboro Bridge; Hell Gate Bridge.

Athens Square Park

http://www.athenssquarepark.org

When you walk through any part of New York City, you will invariably pass by a number of parks of all sizes, places where folks can sit for a moment or a while and kids can play on *City* installed playground structures. Each borough has at least one signature large park, be it Van Cortlandt Park in The Bronx, Prospect Park in Brooklyn, Flushing Meadows-Corona Park in Queens or the centerpiece of them all, Central Park in Manhattan. But each borough also contains many other modest parks, some even inspired by the particular neighborhood in which they stand. One very unique park right in my back yard of Astoria, Queens, is *Athens Square Park*, located on 30th Avenue, between 29th and 30th Streets.

Giving a special nod to the huge Greek population in Astoria (an area sometimes referred to as "*Athens West*"), this small park, which is adjacent to P.S. 17 and includes a children's playground in the rear of the lot, contains four (4) statues and a Doric Column section. As you walk by, through the generally bustling foot and car traffic that defines the 30th Avenue shopping district, you might be surprised by the bronze images spread out in this small area. The incongruous nature of the sculptures goes away quickly, though, when you walk inside the park and check out the celebrated citizens of *Athens Square Park.*

At the entrance, standing on a grand pedestal, is Athena, the patroness of Athens, who in ancient Greek literature is portrayed as the astute companion of heroes, the patron goddess of heroic endeavor. Inside the park, a bust of Aristotle and a seated Socrates (who seems to be holding court), two noted Greek philosophers, join the noted Greek playwright Sophocles, all spread out around the Doric Column centerpiece.

In 1963, this .9-acre site was acquired for a playground, operated jointly by the Parks Department and the Board of Education. A new school and playground were built, and P.S. 17, called the Henry David Thoreau School, for the American naturalist and philosopher (1812-62), welcomed its first pupils in 1967. The addition of Greek statues began with the preaching Socrates in 1993, followed by the Doric Column in 1996, the majestic Athena in 1998, the Aristotle bust in 2008 and finally, a standing Sophocles in 2015. *Athens Square Park* is a wonderful place to simply sit down, as the sound of children playing in the background fuels the ancients in bronze.

The N and W trains to the 30th Avenue station in Astoria/Long Island City leave you one block from *Athens Square Park*. The Q18 and the Q102 buses both run right by the park.

Walking Distance: Noguchi Museum & Socrates Sculpture Park.

B.B. King's

http://www.bbkingblues.com

There are so many entertainment venues in New York City, it seems almost unfair to rate them. Madison Square Garden, the Apollo Theater, Carnegie Hall, the Beacon Theater and the Coney Island Amphitheater are all great places to watch a concert. But for live music in a really intimate venue, I would offer up *B.B. King's Blues Club and Grill* in Times Square as a must go-to for anyone. Opening in 2000 in the heart of Times Square, New York's *B.B. King's* was the third one in the country, after the flagship site in Memphis (1991) and the second club in Los Angeles (1994). In the main room, concerts by living legends like Chuck Berry, Jerry Lee Lewis and Little Richard intertwine nicely with other acts that have been around for a moment or a while, as well as many tribute bands that echo the sounds of a particular group or artist.

The main room at *B.B. King's Blues Club and Grill* is open from 11 AM to 1 AM, as is *Lucille's Grill*, a separate bar and restaurant on the premises which presents up and coming or lesser known acts at lunch time and in prime time. *Lucille's*, named after *B.B. King's* classic guitar, has the feel of a small blues or jazz club; the main room at *B.B King's* has more of a night club look. Either room is a great place to see a show and eat from a very eclectic menu.

One of the staples at *B.B. King's* is the weekend brunches, where an all-you-can-eat buffet complements a targeted performance. The *Beatles Brunch* each Saturday takes you through the history of the Fab Four, as performed by a long time tribute band, Strawberry Fields. And the *Sunday Gospel Brunch* brings the Harlem Gospel Choir downtown for a rousing revival that does indeed fill the soul. Both of these weekly performances are highly recommended. But as with the regular shows, seating is first come, first served, so getting to the club early is a good idea. The food at the club has a slight

Southern twinge, in deference to its Mississippi-bred namesake. The main room is available for private parties of up to 550 people or for cocktail receptions of up to 1,000 attendees. *Lucille's* is available for smaller parties. A decade and a half in, a night at *B.B. King's Blues Club and Grill* is has become a great New York thing, a place everyone should really find the time to visit.

The A, C and E trains to 42nd Street/Port Authority and the 1, 2, 3, N, Q, R and S trains to 42nd Street/Times Square all leave you a half block from *B.B. King's.*

Walking Distance: Madame Tussaud's Wax Museum; Ripley's Believe It or Not Odditorium; New Victory Theater; Port Authority Bus Terminal; Hard Rock Café, New York; Circle Line; Intrepid Sea, Air & Space Museum; Signature Theatre Company; Broadway Theater District; The Town Hall; Bryant Park; New York Public Library; Grand Central Terminal; Amy's Bread; Gulliver's Gate.

Bronx Zoo

http://bronxzoo.com

New York City has a plethora of attractions that cater to and fascinate children of all ages. Arguably the very best of them is the world famous *Bronx Zoo,* located on 265 acres of *The City's* northernmost borough. For a young child making their first visit or an unapologetic adult returning for the first time in decades, the *Bronx Zoo* is an enchanting walk through wildlife in the midst of the concrete that defines all things New York City.

In 1895, a group, made up predominantly of members of the Boone and Crockett Club, founded the New York Zoological Society, which was later renamed the Wildlife Conservation Society, the current overseers of the *Bronx Zoo.* They realized their goal of founding a zoo and promoting the study of zoology when the *Bronx Zoo,* once also known as the *Bronx Zoological Park* and/or the *Bronx Zoological Gardens,* opened to the public on November 8, 1899. The original zoo offered up 843 animals, featured in 22 exhibits. Those numbers would grow in the next century and the *Bronx Zoo* became the largest metropolitan zoo in the United States and one of the biggest in the world.

Among the exhibits that currently are accessible with a general admission ticket are the Baboon Reserve, the Himalayan Highlands, Madagascar!, the Mouse House, the Aquatic Bird House, Tiger Mountain, the World of Birds, the World of Reptiles, the Zoo Center and the Bison Range. There are also premium exhibits. You can pay $5 apiece for these particular attractions or simply get a Total Access pass, which gives you the run of the park, so to speak. The premium exhibits include the Bug Carousel, the Children's Zoo, the Congo Gorilla Forest and the 4-D Theater. It is useful to note that General Admission is free on Wednesdays, making it the busiest day each week and the destination day for all New York City children's camps in the Summer.

A giant map at each entrance gate and a paper version that is given to every visitor help plan the routes that one might take in exploring the vast hills of the *Bronx Zoo.* In addition, throughout the yard, there are directional signposts at intersections which use the coordinates of the paper map to help you navigate the park. These tools help lessen the chances of being turned around as you weave in and out of exhibits. The *Bronx Zoo* is, without question, a New York classic.

The 2 train to Pelham Parkway leaves you near the *Bronx Zoo's* Bronx River entrance. The BxM11 express bus also goes to the Bronx River entrance and the Bx9 and Bx19 buses to 183rd and Southern Boulevard leave you at the *Zoo's* Southern Boulevard pedestrian entrance.

Walking Distance: Bronx Park; Bronx River Art Center.

Bryant Park

http://www.bryantpark.org

Sitting on land that possesses one of the most interesting tales in New York City history, *Bryant Park* today is one of the most enjoyable stops in the heart of *The City* to sit down, take a break and momentarily escape the concrete jungle that it sits in the midst of. Most of those who find themselves relaxing in this small but vibrant tract of land would be surprised and even inspired by what has transpired there in the past few centuries.

Located on 6th Avenue between 40th and 42nd Streets, the area now known as *Bryant Park* was deemed public property by Colonial Governor Thomas Dongan in the year 1686. In 1822, fifteen years after the grid of streets in Manhattan was created, the City of New York gained jurisdiction to the land and made it a potter's field one year later. This lasted until 1840, when it was decommissioned in preparation for the construction of the Croton Reservoir, which stood (from 1842-1900) where the Main Branch of the New York City Library now resides. Now called *Reservoir Square*, the former potter's field re-emerged in the mid-1850's, with the *New York Crystal Palace* and 315-foot high *Latting Observatory* forming the *Crystal Palace Exhibit*, one of the first major tourism sites in New York City history. The exhibit closed in 1854. During the Civil War, *Reservoir Square* was used as an encampment for Union Army troops.

In 1884, *Reservoir Square* was renamed *Bryant Park*, in honor of the longtime editor of the New York Evening Post, poet William Cullen Bryant, who had died a few years earlier. In the ensuing decades, *Bryant Park* saw a few renovations, including a period in the 1920's when the north end of the park was closed as the Interborough Rapid Transit (IRT) subway tunneled below. A design by Queens' architect Lusby Simpson was implemented by new Parks Commissioner Robert Moses in 1934. In 1975, the park was named a

"Scenic Landmark," though by the late 70's, drug dealers had become more prevalent in the park. Fortunately, by 1992, the dealers had moved on and yet another renovation had left the park much as it is today, with more entranceways a new amenity.

These days, *Bryant Park* features film festivals in the Summer and a Winter Village, complete with an ice rink, in the Winter. A slew of holiday gifts shops added at Christmastime offer up some of the most eclectic shopping in *The City.*

The B, D, F and M trains to 42nd Street/Bryant Park leave you at the entrance to the park. In addition, all trains to 42nd Street/Times Square and Grand Central Terminal leave you a few blocks from Bryant Park.

Walking Distance: New York Public Library; Grand Central Terminal; The Town Hall; B.B. King's; Madame Tussaud's Wax Museum; Ripley's Believe It or Not Odditorium; New Victory Theater; Port Authority Bus Terminal; Hard Rock Café, Broadway Theater District; Carolines on Broadway; Morgan Library & Museum; St. Patrick's Cathedral; Gulliver's Gate.

Carolines on Broadway

http://www.carolines.com

In the late 1970's and all through the 1980's, comedy clubs were prominent and thriving in *The City.* Names like *Catch a Rising Star, Who's on First?* and *Dangerfield's* (run by legendary comedian Rodney Dangerfield) became household words for many New Yorkers. In the 90's, the comedy club scene began to dry up and today, there are just a few relevant ones still out there. One iconic club that has weathered the times is *Carolines on Broadway*, which was originally in Chelsea and later located in the South Street Seaport district. In 1992, *Carolines* moved from the Seaport to 1626 Broadway, between 49th and 50th Streets, with the lengthened and geographically accurate moniker, *Carolines on Broadway.*

Caroline Hirsch opened up shop in Chelsea in 1982, originally as a small cabaret club, with comedians among the acts booked. Appearances by future legends like Jerry Seinfeld, Tim Allen, Billy Crystal and Rosie O'Donnell helped make stand-up comedy the main attraction and assumed the singular focus that *Carolines* would take on. The need for a larger space spurred the move to the South Street Seaport district, which proved very lucrative. A television audience also arrived with the birth of the A&E Network's "*Carolines Comedy Hour*," which was filmed at the club and would earn a *Cable ACE Award* for "Best Comedy Series." In 1992, Hirsch moved *Carolines* one more time, to its current home on Broadway.

Today, *Carolines on Broadway* is most justified in its claim to being "America's Premier Comedy Nightclub," based on tenure and the continuing number of current top of the line comics who play the 300-seat room in the heart of New York City's theater district. *Carolines on Broadway* also produces the yearly *New York Comedy Festival*, a five-day event in which some of the best comedy talent around appears not only at *Carolines,* but also at other iconic venues like the Beacon Theatre, the Apollo Theater and Madison Square Garden. Various fund raisers and benefits are also a staple on *Carolines'* yearly calendar. These include yearly events for the *Ms. Foundation* and for the *Ovarian Cancer Research Fund*, which honors the late comic genius, Madeline Kahn. Overall, a night at *Carolines on Broadway* is sure to send you home laughing, whether you see an established comic or a group of up and coming funny men and women at one of *Carolines*' New Talent shows.

The N, R and Q trains to 49th Street, the 1, C and E trains to 50th Street and the B, D, F and M trains to 47th-50th Rockefeller Center all leave you within a few blocks of *Caroline's on Broadway.* The M7 and M50 buses also have stops within walking distance of the club.

Walking Distance: Broadway Theater District; B.B. King's; Madame Tussaud's Wax Museum; Ripley's Believe It or Not Odditorium; New Victory Theater; Hard Rock Café; Port Authority Bus Terminal; Rockefeller Center; Radio City Music Hall; St. Patrick's Cathedral; The Meatball Shop; Amy's Bread; Gulliver's Gate.

Circle Line

https://www.circleline42.com

Among the many interesting experiences that you can have in New York City, taking the *Circle Line* is definitely one of the most "*New York Things*" that one can do. A morning, afternoon or early evening spent on the waterways that flow around Manhattan, the other boroughs and New Jersey is a most fascinating way to see *The City.*

The *Circle Line* began running boat tours around Manhattan in 1945 and more than 70 years later, different length cruises offered today by the *Circle Line* provide a most unique snapshot of *The City.* The only cruise company in New York Harbor exclusively dedicated to sightseeing, the *Circle Line* fleet is specifically designed to let you see as much as possible in any weather. The steel vessels, featuring huge windows on two levels, provide a comfortable setting, 12 months a year. And when the weather is good, outside seating at the rear of each boat gives customers a magnificent look and feel for the area.

Besides the most famous cruise, the 2½-hour "*Best of NYC Cruise*," which circles Manhattan Island completely, there is a 1½-hour "*Landmarks Cruise*," a 2-hour "*Landmarks and Brooklyn Cruise*" and a 1-hour "*Liberty Cruise*." All four of these originate in the daytime. A special 2-hour "*Harbor Lights Cruise*" runs in the early evening on weekends. And there are a few once-a-year jaunts, the 2-hour "*St. Patrick's Day Cruise*," the 4½-hour "*July 4th Fireworks Cruise*" and the 3-hour "*New Year's Eve Cruise*," which give those holidays a most unique perspective. Seasonal 8-hour "*Bear Mountain Cruises,*" which go all the way up the Hudson River, round out the many ways one can enjoy a *Circle Line* tour. Each cruise has a guide who takes you through the tour, pointing out landmarks along the way.

For those who went on a *Circle Line* cruise as a child many years ago, like me, the most vivid difference today is technology-driven. The ships are pretty much the same, but the advances in the photography industry are more relevant to this type of sightseeing than any other. Digital cameras and cell phone cameras, with the capability of taking prodigious amounts of pictures, make it much more likely to get superb photos, as opposed to decades ago, when you really needed to consider each shot, because your camera roll held a finite number of exposures. In any case, the *Circle Line* is unquestionably the best venue to take photos of *The City* from.

The A, C, E, 1,2, 3, 7, N, R, Q and W trains to their 42nd Street stations leave you four or five blocks from Pier 83, the home of the *Circle Line* on 42nd Street and 12th Avenue, depending on where you exit the station.

Walking Distance: Signature Theatre Company; B.B. King's; Madame Tussaud's Wax Museum; Ripley's Believe It or Not Odditorium; New Victory Theater; Port Authority Bus Terminal; Hard Rock Café; Amy's Bread; Broadway Theater District.

Dangerfield's

http://dangerfields.com

The greatest lasting legacy of the comedy club boom of the late 1970's and 1980's is a nightclub named after one of the most famous comedians of all-time. *Dangerfield's*, located at 1118 First Avenue, off 61st Street, is the "*longest running comedy club in the world*," as their website reminds you. The club opened in 1969, even before the man himself found his greatest fame.

To a few generations, Rodney Dangerfield was a fan favorite and one of the most unique comics ever. The bug-eyed, red tied, boisterous galoot who lived off the mantra "*No Respect*," was a star of television, movies and stand-up comedy live. Born Jacob Cohen in Deer Park, Long Island in 1922, he had a tough upbringing, as his father abandoned the family when young Jacob was just a kid. His family moved to Kew Gardens, Queens and he wrote material for stand-ups as early as age 15. He changed his name to Jack Roy and tried unsuccessfully to foster a career in entertainment in the early 1960's. His big breakthrough came when he took on a character's name from the Jack Benny radio show of the 1940's and morphed it into a persona that would define his career.

Rodney Dangerfield in the Benny sketches was a cowboy star who received little respect from the outside world. This was the inspiration for the Rodney Dangerfield that would make his first big splash as a last second fill-in on the Ed Sullivan Show in March of 1967. More spots on Sullivan led to headlining in Las Vegas and eventually making 35 appearances on The Tonight Show with Johnny Carson, where, like many other comics, he really became a star. His 1980 album, "*No Respect*," received a Grammy. This led to movies like Caddyshack (1980), Easy Money (1983) and Back to School (1986) and a memorable string of "Lite Beer from Miller" TV commercials.

Along the way, Rodney opened *Dangerfield's* in 1969 with his friend, Anthony Bevacqua and it became a great venue for headlining comics like George Carlin, Sam Kinison and Chris Rock. *Dangerfield's* was also used for popular HBO specials, including one which heralded new comedians, which is ironic, since the club does not have amateur or open mic nights on its schedule, to this day. Before he died in 2004, Rodney could often be found at the bar of his club, as the show went on in the other room. Tony Bevacqua still runs the club.

The N, Q, R, 4, 5 and 6 trains to 59th Street/Lexington Avenue and the F train to Lexington Avenue/63rd Street all leave you a short walk from *Dangerfield's*. The M15, M31 or M57 buses all stop nearby, as well.

Walking Distance: Mount Vernon Hotel Museum; Roosevelt Island Tramway; 59th Street Bridge

Film Forum

http://filmforum.org

One of the things that I have stressed to people about New York City is that some of the greatest places to go to are relatively small or modest in scope. The idea that less is more can be a reality, even in the *Big City*. Maybe the most vibrant example of this is the *Film Forum* at 209 West Houston Street. For almost 60 years, this otherwise ordinary little theater company has offered up some of the most thought-provoking films, both past and present.

If you want to speak of grass roots beginnings, consider that *Film Forum*, when it first arrived in 1970, consisted of 50 folding chairs and one projector. Conceived as an alternate space for independent and foreign films, the *Film Forum* took a rather circuitous route to its current location. In 1975, under director Karen Cooper, it moved downtown to the Vandam Theater, before Cooper oversaw the construction of a twin cinema on Watts Street. In 1989, the Watts Street cinema was demolished by developers, which ultimately led the *Film Forum* to West Houston Street, which one could argue is a perfect home for such a New York venue.

These days, the *Film Forum* consists of three screens and is open 365 days a year. Two specific film programs are adhered to and form the basis of the operation on West Houston. One is dedicated to the New York City theatrical premieres of independent and foreign art films. The second, first instituted in 1987, offers repertory selections, including foreign and American classics, different genres, directors' retrospectives and festival screenings. Extended runs of favorites from both of these programs are played on the third screen, as well as some new films. One of the few autonomously run cinemas in the United States and the only one in New York City, *Film Forum* has shown continuous growth and success through the years.

One of the fun things about the Film Forum is that the lobby is alive with what the place is all about. Advertisements and reviews of current films showing are presented on free-standing easels just inside the door, with more about these and future films lining the walls leading to the three cinema halls. On Sundays at 11 AM, they hold the popular *Classics for Kids and Their Families* program. In addition, the classic films that are regularly added to the mix are generally re-mastered and upgraded versions.

The 1 train to Houston Street and the A, B, C, D, E, F and M trains to the West 4th Street/Washington Square station all leave you a few blocks from the *Film Forum* on West Houston Street. The M5 bus stops right by the theater.

Walking Distance: IFC Center; Washington Square Park; Triangle Shirtwaist Factory site; Merchant's House Museum; Ukrainian Museum; New Museum; The Basilica at Old St. Patrick's Cathedral.

Flatiron Building

http://www.freetoursbyfoot.com/flatiron-district-nyc

Of all the famous New York City skyscrapers, the one that may well be the most unique and certainly most accessible for photography, is the iconic *Flatiron Building*, located at 175 Fifth Avenue. The odd, triangular-shaped building, whose name comes from its resemblance to a cast-iron clothes iron, has long been a most preferred tourist site, as taking a photo there can offer proof that you were in the heart of New York City.

Bordered by Fifth Avenue, Broadway and East 22nd Street, the 22-story structure was, upon its completion in 1902, one of only two skyscrapers north of 14th Street, the other being the Metropolitan Life Insurance Company Tower. William Eno, whose father Amos had owned the land for over 40 years when he passed away in 1899, sold the site in 1901 to the Cumberland Realty Company, an investment partnership created by Harry S. Black, the CEO of the skyscraper building Fuller Company. Black intended to construct a new headquarters building on the site, despite the recent deterioration of the surrounding Madison Square neighborhood. He hired Chicago architect Daniel Burnham, who fashioned a vertical Renaissance palazzo with Beaux-Art styling. The building was slated to be called *The Fuller Building*, after the recently deceased (1900) founder of the Fuller Company, George A. Fuller, who was known as the "*father of the skyscraper*." Unfortunately, the locals had gotten used to calling the site "*The Flatiron*"' due to the shape of the block and thus Burnham's creation would always be called the *Flatiron Building*, first unofficially, and eventually once and for all. During construction of the *Flatiron*, when the winds swirling around the sharp corners of the building would blow ladies' dresses up, the police took to shooing lecherous men toward 23rd street by yelling "*23 Skidoo*."

Originally occupied by magazine, vanity and music publishers, as well as small businesses, the *Flatiron* through the years has hosted clothing and toy companies, as well as a famous United Cigar Store at its base, which was replaced by a Walgreens in the 1940's. These days, a brand new hotel has been considered, but would have to wait for tenants' leases to run out in the next few years. The *Flatiron Building* was designated a New York City Landmark in 1966. In 1979, it was added to the National Register of Historic Places and in 1989, it was designated a National Historic Landmark.

The 23rd Street stops of the C, E, F, M, N, R, 1, 4 and 6 trains all leave you either right near the *Flatiron Building,* or just a few avenues away. The M1, M2, M3, M5 and M23 buses to their various 23rd Street stops also stop near the *Flatiron.*

Walking Distance: Museum of Mathematics; Madison Square Park; The Meatball Shop; Irish Repertory Theatre; The Cell Theatre; Theodore Roosevelt Birthplace; The High Line; Union Square Park; Old Town Bar and Restaurant; JJ Hat Center.

Franklin D. Roosevelt Four Freedoms Park

http://www.fdrfourfreedomspark.org/visit

At the southern tip of Roosevelt Island, there exists one of the great contemplative places in New York City. The *Franklin D. Roosevelt Four Freedoms Park*, which pays tribute to a theme from a famous speech made by the 32nd President of the United States, is as fine and understated a memorial as one might find.

The small island located in the East River, between Manhattan and Queens, was known as Blackwell's Island from the late 17th Century until 1921. From 1921-71, an Era when the island was used mainly for hospitals, it was called Welfare Island. In 1971, it was changed again, this time to Roosevelt Island, in honor of the longest tenured President in United States history, who also happened to be a polio survivor. Though conceived soon after the name change, the triangular *Franklin D. Roosevelt Four Freedoms Park* didn't open until 2012.

The famous words of FDR's which are celebrated in *Four Freedoms Park* came as part of his January 6, 1941 State of the Union address. The excerpt that is etched in the back of a large stone tablet in the park articulates these freedoms:

"In the future days, which we seek to make secure, we look forward to a world founded upon four essential human freedoms. The first is freedom of speech and expression -- everywhere in the world. The second is freedom of every person to worship God in his own way -- everywhere in the world. The third is freedom from want... everywhere in the world. The fourth is freedom from fear... anywhere in the world. That is no vision of a distant millennium. It is a definite basis for a kind of world attainable in our own time and generation."

On the front side of the tablet containing these words of President

Roosevelt is a huge and impressive bust of FDR, which is the cornerstone of *Four Freedoms Park*, where a fabulous view of the United Nations, Chrysler and Empire State Buildings can be found. As a bonus, near the entrance to the park stand the ruins of the old *Smallpox Hospital* (1856-1950's). These are the only ruins in New York City on the National Register of Historic Places (1972) and are also a New York City Landmark (1976). The *Four Freedoms Park* is a true New York pleasure.

To F train, the Q102 bus from Queens and the Roosevelt Island Tramway from 59th Street and 2nd Avenue in Manhattan all go to Roosevelt Island. After exiting the bus, Subway or Tram station, you walk south along the waterline to get to the *Franklin D. Roosevelt Four Freedoms Park* at the southernmost tip of the Island.

Walking Distance: Smallpox Hospital ruins; Roosevelt Island Tramway.

Grand Central Terminal

http://www.grandcentralterminal.com

In my travels to ballparks around the country, I have had the added pleasure of visiting a number of classic railway stations. From 30th Street Station in Philadelphia and Penn Station in Baltimore, which are both still active, to Union Station in Denver, which does serve Amtrak, yet is more a tourist site (with shops and a hotel), to Union Station in Omaha, which is now the Durham Museum, a spectacular showpiece of railyards of another time, I have been fascinated by the atmosphere at these once (and still) bustling edifices. Throw in Union Station in St. Louis, once the gateway to the west via locomotive and now a huge mall, and you understand that sometimes hallowed grounds need to be preserved, in one form or another. And back home in New York City, the greatest rail station of them all still resides. Of course, I speak of *Grand Central Terminal*, at 89 East 42nd Street in the heart of Manhattan.

Still called *Grand Central Station* by many, it was built in 1871, with the original building called the *Grand Central Depot*. Following a renovation and expansion in 1901, it became *Grand Central Station.* The third version, unveiled in 1913 and still going strong more than a century later, was dubbed *Grand Central Terminal. Grand Central* was the brainchild of railroad baron Cornelius Vanderbilt, who sought to link four competing railroads of the time—the Hudson River, New York Central, New York & Harlem, and New York & New Haven. During the 1860s, Vanderbilt bought controlling stock in the first three, which created a single rail empire. Today, all four have been united as Metro-North, which took over *Grand Central Terminal* in 1982.

Grand Central Terminal and its crosstown rival, Pennsylvania Station, were once the two grand sites for rail travel in and out of New York City. The architecture of each of these huge hubs was what distinguished them and when Pennsylvania Station's main concourse was demolished in 1963, many feared that *Grand Central* might meet a similar fate. But it survived, given landmark status in 1978. These days, beyond the Metro-North traffic and the subway below, there are some 68 shops and 35 eateries on the *GCT* grounds and the Vanderbilt Hall, in one corner of the terminal, hosts numerous events throughout the year. A walk through *Grand Central Terminal* is a wonderfully hectic ride, though to see the Main Concourse, with its iconic celestial ceiling mural and Grand Central Clock above the information booth, remains a New York treasure.

The 4, 5, 6 and 7 trains stop at *Grand Central Terminal* and the F and M trains to 42nd Street/Bryant Park leave you a few blocks from *Grand Central Terminal.*

Walking Distance: New York Public Library; Bryant Park; The Town Hall; B.B. King's; Madame Tussaud's Wax Museum; Ripley's Believe It or Not Odditorium; New Victory Theater; Port Authority Bus Terminal; Hard Rock Café, Broadway Theater District; Carolines on Broadway; Morgan Library & Museum; St. Patrick's Cathedral; Gulliver's Gate.

Gulliver's Gate

https://gulliversgate.co

A wonderful artistic display has arrived in the Times Square area which really must be seen. Using multiple teams of sculptors from around the world, *Gulliver's Gate* is an amazing walk through the Planet Earth, through the scope of detailed miniatures. Located at 216 West 44th Street, *Gulliver's Gate* is one of the most unique displays ever. Even in the largesse that is New York City, the scope of the miniature world that is *Gulliver's Gate* is huge.

Named for the 18th Century Jonathan Swift novel Gulliver's Travels, about a man who at one point enters a world of miniature people called Lilliputians, the goal of *Gulliver's Gate* appears to be that of re-creating the world at 1.87 scale, or .8 inches for a 6-foot person. When it opened on May 8th, the United States and New York, of course, were big parts of the presentation, but Europe, Asia, Africa and Australia are also well represented, including places that most of us have only a mind's eye view of. The beauty of *Gulliver's Gate* is in the detail and the layout of each section of the world.

Eiran Gazit, the President & CEO of Gulliver's Gate, was the founder and first CEO of Mini Israel, a 14-acre miniature display outside of Jerusalem. Along with Co-Founder & VP of Development Michael Langer and an eclectic team of planners, artists and techno-wizards, Gazit helped make *Gulliver's Gate* a reality. Yoni Shapira, the brother-in-law of my friend and former NYC Transit co-worker Filip Luks, worked with Gazit on Mini Israel and is one of the creators of the Jerusalem section of *Gulliver's Gate*. Models were crafted by creative teams all over the world, before being shipped to the United States for installation in *Gulliver's Gate.*

Beyond the disparate sites, which include the Brooklyn Bridge, the Colosseum in Rome, epic towers in Malaysia and Singapore and the Taj Mahal, there are a number of interactive effects, like the Northern Lights, which are set off by using a souvenir key that each visitor is given (to keep). There is also a photographic chamber where visitors can be scanned and made into a citizen of *Gulliver's Gate* and also afforded the opportunity to purchase three different sizes of exact replicas of themselves, created by a 3D printer. And a working airport, where planes will take-off and land, is currently being built. Upon arrival, *Gulliver's Gate* instantly became yet another special site to visit in New York City.

The A, C and E trains to 42nd Street/Port Authority and the 1, 2, 3, N, Q, R and S trains to 42nd Street/Times Square all leave you a few blocks from *Gulliver's Gate.,* on 44th Street between 7th and 8th Avenues.

Walking Distance: New York Public Library; Bryant Park; The Town Hall; Grand Central Terminal; B.B. King's; Madame Tussaud's Wax Museum; Ripley's Believe It or Not Odditorium; New Victory Theater; Port Authority Bus Terminal; Hard Rock Café, Broadway Theater District; Carolines on Broadway; Amy's Bread; Morgan Library & Museum; St. Patrick's Cathedral.

Hall of Fame for Great Americans

http://www.bcc.cuny.edu/halloffame/?page=home

Among the fairly unheralded sites in New York City, arguably the most impressive is the *Hall of Fame for Great Americans*, located on the Bronx Community College campus. A visit to this site is an absolute joy, rich with history and reminders of so many people who helped form and give growth to the fledgling United States. Voted for between 1900 and 1976, the *Hall of Fame for Great Americans* is a shrine to the foundation of America.

The idea for such a Hall of Fame was originated by Dr. Henry Mitchell MacCracken, Chancellor of New York University from 1891 to 1910. The first "Hall of Fame" of any kind in the country, it was designed by one of the great architects of his time, Stanford White. The Hall consists of 98 busts in a winding 630-foot Colonnade. Three adjoining buildings, the Colonnade-Gould Memorial Library, the Hall of Languages, and Cornelius Baker Hall of Philosophy, were also designed by White and complement the Colonnade. The *Hall of Fame for Great Americans* was dedicated on May 30, 1901, right in the middle of the construction of the Hall of Languages (1894), the Gould Memorial Library (1899), and Philosophy Hall (1912).

The busts of the honorees are situated in categories like Statesmen, Teachers, Authors, Scientists and Soldiers. As you walk through the *Hall*, each bust is accompanied by a brief quote made by the person immortalized in bronze. Naturally, a number of U.S. Presidents are represented, including George Washington, Abraham Lincoln, Ulysses S. Grant and Theodore and Franklin D. Roosevelt. Founding Fathers Benjamin Franklin and Alexander Hamilton are prominent, as are Civil War icons Robert E. Lee and William Tecumseh Sherman. There are celebrated authors, such as Mark Twain, Edgar Allan Poe and Henry Wadsworth Longfellow and notable inventors like Thomas Edison, Robert Fulton and George Washington Carver. And though most of the names are well known, there are some that are not as familiar to the general public and just seeing these busts, of people like Lillian Wald, Mark Hopkins and Asa Gray, gives one the impetus to do some research and learn more about these people and how they contributed to America. That may well be the most important part of going to see the *Hall of Fame for Great Americans.* Any place that is a catalyst to the mind is somewhere that people should see. You only need a valid photo ID to enter the BCC campus and visit the *Hall.*

.The 4 train to Burnside Avenue leaves you a short walk to the *Hall of Fame for Great Americans* in Bronx Community College. The BX 3 bus stops right by the BCC campus.

Walking Distance: Bronx Community College; Francis Martin Library; Roberto Clemente State Park

Hard Rock Café, New York

http://www.hardrock.com/cafes/new-york

The first great theme bar/restaurant chain ever conceived was the *Hard Rock Café*, which began in London in 1971 and first appeared on the New York scene in 1984. In the ensuing years, the *Hard Rock* brand has been one of the most respected and admired, for both the good food and the signature atmosphere in each of the cafes, hotels and casinos that bear the *Hard Rock* name. One of the earliest and most popular venues to come out of this huge chain was the *Hard Rock Café, New York.*

Americans Peter Morton and Isaac Tigrett opened the first *Hard Rock Café* in Piccadilly, London in 1971. The signature rock and roll memorabilia that would define the walls of every *Hard Rock* would be adopted in short order. Morton had graduated from the University of Denver in 1969, with a B.S.B.A. in restaurant & hotel management. Tigrett would later partner with actor Dan Aykroyd to open the House of Blues chain in 1992. Both Morton and Tigrett would eventually sell their *Hard Rock* interests to the London-based Rank Organization, who would in turn sell most of the *Hard Rock* properties to the Seminole Tribe of Florida, the current owners.

The *Hard Rock Café, New York*, opened on April 12, 1984, on 57th Street, just off Broadway, as the fifth one in existence, following those in London, Toronto, Los Angeles and Roppongi, Japan. The original New York site featured the iconic back end of a '57 Cadillac hanging out of the wall above the entrance. With the closing of the Los Angeles *Hard Rock* in 2006, the *Hard Rock Café, New York*, which moved to its current location on the corner of 43rd Street and Broadway in Times Square on August 12, 2005, is the oldest of the 64 currently operating in the United States. There are almost 200 *Hard Rocks* in the world, from the United States, Canada, Mexico, Central and South America, the Caribbean, Europe, Asia, the Middle East, Africa and the Pacific Rim.

The *Hard Rock Café, New York* in Times Square features a great souvenir Rock Shop, which serves as the main entrance, with the restaurant one level below. Rock memorabilia is everywhere and one can be entertained simply by walking all around the premises while waiting for your meal, or after you're finished. You can also rent out the *Hard Rock* catering halls within the building for parties of all sizes. The *Hard Rock Café, New York* is a must-see eating/ entertainment establishment in *The City*.

The 1, 2, 3, N, Q, R and S trains to 42nd Street/Times Square all leave you a block away from the *Hard Rock Café, New York* on the corner of 43rd Street and Broadway.

Walking Distance: Madame Tussaud's Wax Museum; Ripley's Believe It or Not Odditorium; New Victory Theater; B.B. King's; Port Authority Bus Terminal; Intrepid Sea, Air & Space Museum; Circle Line; Signature Theatre Company; Broadway Theater District; Carolines on Broadway; The Town Hall; Bryant Park; New York Public Library; Grand Central Terminal; Amy's Bread; Gulliver's Gate.

Holiday Train Show at the New York Botanical Garden

http://www.nybg.org/home

New York City is an especially glorious place to traipse through during the Holiday season. The Rockefeller Center Christmas Tree, the Radio City Music Hall Christmas Show right down the block from that tree and the plethora of fabulous window displays, led by the legendary Macy's Herald Square windows, are among the most popular destinations. Up in The Bronx, though, at the *New York Botanical Garden,* there's another special New York happening each Christmas season. The *Holiday Train Show,* which has brought absolute joy and wonderment to generations, celebrated its 25th year in 2016 and remains one of the signature go-to sites in *The City* each December.

The *Holiday Train Show* today includes 150 landmarks that are amazingly re-created using bark, leaves, and other natural materials. Famous sites, like the Brooklyn Bridge, Yankee Stadium, St. Patrick's Cathedral, the Statue of Liberty and the New York Public Library meld with lesser known historic venues like the Dyckman Farmhouse and the Morris-Jumel Mansion to form a broad mosaic of *The City.* Displayed in a multi-room greenhouse – the Enid A. Haupt Conservatory – this panorama of sites provides the foundation for the G-scale locomotives that twist in and around the landmarks. The *Holiday Train Show* is a truly remarkable sight to see in person, though it is not right out in the open, like most other New York City holiday exhibitions. Still, I believe that all of those who make the trip up to The Bronx to see the *Holiday Train Show* will come back with a genuinely festive feeling inside.

The *New York Botanical Garden,* which celebrated its 125th year in 2016, was granted National Historic Landmark status in 1967. At

250 acres, it is the largest botanical garden residing in any city in the United States. Any day spent at the massive *NYBG* is enjoyable, yet at Christmas time, the events presented there are the most far-reaching to the general public. In addition to the very popular *Holiday Train Show*, they have holiday a cappella singing in the visitor's center, holiday movie screenings and harmony concerts in the Ross Hall auditorium and various children's activities throughout the grounds. The *Holiday Train Show* yearly garners a huge daily turnout, so buying tickets early is probably a good idea, as they sell specifically-timed entrance fees online, to keep the large crowd spread out, yet flowing.

To get to the *New York Botanical Garden* and the *Holiday Train Show* therein, take the D train to the Bedford Park Boulevard stop and walk 8 short blocks. If you don't want to walk that far, the Bx26 bus stops by the train station and at the *Garden's* Mosholu Gate entrance.

Walking Distance: Fordham University.

IFC Center

http://www.ifccenter.com

The growth of cable television in the 1980's spawned many new networks and all levels of entertainment. Arguably the most influential artistic entity that arrived with the dawn of 1,000 channels came in the form of the independent film networks, like the Independent Film Channel and the Sundance Channel. And though they existed before, theaters that screened and promoted the world of independent film took on a new importance, much less underground, let's say. One of the best of the new cinemas to grace the scene opened in 2005, when the *IFC Center* set up shop on the site of one of the great old movie houses in New York City, the *Waverly Theater.*

The *IFC Center*, located at 323 Sixth Avenue in Greenwich Village, sits in a wonderful intersection that once featured the familiar *Waverly* marquee. The *Waverly Theater* was a place that drew substance not only from the features it played, but the area in which it stood. That intangible joy that one got when going to the *Waverly* is at least partially present these days, outside and within the *IFC Center.* The *IFC Center* features five state-of-the-art cinemas, with Dolby Digital 5.1 surround sound and 3D capability. Many theatrical premieres of independent and foreign films and documentaries play in the various-sized screening halls at the *IFC Center.* Though there are a few other theaters dedicated to independent film in New York City, the *IFC Center* is the most expansive and far-reaching, going beyond just the movies themselves.

At the *IFC Center*, they have a number of special programs, such as *DOC NYC*, the country's largest documentary festival, held each November. In the Spring, Fall and Winter, they hold the *Stranger Than Fiction* documentary series. A monthly program called *Queer/Art/Film* is chaired by LGBTQ guest curators. And two bookending time-oriented themes, the *Weekend Classics*, held at 11 AM, on

Friday through Sunday and the *Waverly Midnights*, featuring cult movies on Fridays and Saturdays at Midnight, offer up plenty of laughs and/or memories for all who attend. Vintage movie posters, known as the *Posteritati Gallery at IFC Center*, adorn the walls of the upper level. Organic popcorn and gourmet snacks are served in the refreshment stand. At the *IFC Center*, it is not just movie watching, but experiencing film, that seizes the day. A membership in the *IFC Center* exposes one to a number of discounts, screenings and previews.

The A, B, C, D, E, F and M trains to the West 4th Street/ Washington Square station stop right across from the *IFC Center* at 323 Sixth Avenue. The 1 train to Christopher Street/Sheridan Square leaves you a few blocks away. The M5 bus stops right by the theater.

Walking Distance: Film Forum; The Meatball Shop; Washington Square Park; Triangle Shirtwaist Factory site; Merchant's House Museum; Ukrainian Museum; New Museum; The Basilica at Old St. Patrick's Cathedral.

Irish Repertory Theatre

https://irishrep.org

Among all the fabulous Off-Broadway theatre companies, there is one that touches me closest to the heart. The *Irish Repertory Theatre*, which has been located on 22nd Street, between Sixth and Seventh Avenues, since 1995, is a haven for the works of both classic and modern day Irish and Irish-American playwrights.

Founded in 1988 by Ciaran O'Reilly and Charlotte Moore, their first production was of Sean O'Casey's "*The Plough and the Stars.*" In the ensuing three decades, the *Irish Repertory Theatre* has put on over 125 plays and musicals which live true to Moore and O'Reilly's original mission of bringing works by Irish and Irish-American masters and contemporary playwrights to American audiences. Helping form an understanding of the contemporary Irish-American experience and encouraging the development of new works about the Irish and Irish-American experience are also mandates of the *IRT,* though other cultures are in the mix at times.

Through the years, the *Irish Repertory Theatre* has given *The City* a number of memorable productions, with some of the best singing and musical accompaniment found on or Off-Broadway. They have also delighted the local crowd by bringing back favorite works in different seasons, including Frank McCourt's "*The Irish... and How They Got That Way,*" which ran four times from its debut in 1998 through 2010 and Dylan Thomas' "*A Child's Christmas in Wales,*" which ran nine times through 2016. Works by Irish originals like W.B. Yeats and Oscar Wilde and revivals of "*Finian's Rainbow*" by legendary composer Yip Harburg ("Over the Rainbow," "Brother, Can You Spare a Dime") all form the foundation for pieces by more contemporary playwrights. The *IRT* used alternate New York sites in 2014-15, while their base on 22nd Street was being renovated. Back home in 2016-17, with a new and improved Francis Greenburger

Mainstage and an updated W. Scott Lucas Studio Theatre downstairs, the *Irish Repertory Theatre* looks to be a New York fixture for many years to come.

The *Irish Repertory Theatre* also produces some specialty programs, like James Joyce's "*The Dead, 1904*," which was presented in 2016, with 40 audience guests a night taking part in the Irish dinner party that the play is set within. The American Irish Historical Society, a nineteenth-century mansion overlooking Central Park, was used to help replicate this period piece. The *Irish Repertory Theatre* provides an enjoyable night at the theatre for all, whether you're Irish or not.

The 23rd Street stops of the C, E, F, M, N, Q, R, W, 1, 4 and 6 trains all leave you within a few blocks of the *Irish Repertory Theatre* at 132 West 22nd Street. The various 23rd Street stops on the M5, M6, M7 and M23 buses also leave you right nearby.

Walking Distance: Museum of Mathematics; Madison Square Park; Flatiron Building; The Meatball Shop; The Cell Theatre; Theodore Roosevelt Birthplace; The High Line; Union Square Park; Old Town Bar and Restaurant; JJ Hat Center.

Jane's Carousel

http://janescarousel.com

Wherever land and water meet, the chances of great things happening seem to multiply. Along the shorelines of New York's five boroughs, I have found this is often the case. And in a wonderful place called *Brooklyn Bridge Park*, this is particularly true. Inside this modest park lies a piece of artistic history, one that can be shared by children of all ages, as the circus marquees say. In all of New York City, there is nothing, based on location, presentation and historical significance, quite like *Jane's Carousel.*

Jane Walentas, an artist in *DUMBO*, began restoring what would become *Jane's Carousel* in the mid-1980's. Created in 1922 by the Philadelphia Toboggan Company and originally installed in *Idora Park* in Youngston, Ohio, Jane and her husband David purchased the entire carousel at auction in 1984, which prevented it from being sold off in separate lots. In her *DUMBO* studio, Jane scraped and re-painted the 48 horses and 2 chariots of the carousel, with small beveled mirrors on the bridles and delicate pin-striping also restored and re-painted, along with running boards, scenery panels and structural pieces. Fully restored and set under a glass pavilion created by architect Jean Nouvel, the newly christened *Jane's Carousel* opened to the public in September of 2011 inside *Brooklyn Bridge Park.*

Approaching the *Nouvel Pavilion* and *Jane's Carousel* within, one can get a sense of somehow walking into a children's story book. The view of the carousel from the Manhattan Bridge side of the park, with the Brooklyn Bridge and the Lower Manhattan skyline in the background, is one of the most awe-inspiring in *The City*, which is saying a lot. This is true, whether in early afternoon or at dusk, where the moon off the East River often enhances the view. *Jane's Carousel* is opened 6 days a week in the Summer and 4 days a week in the Winter. Birthday parties, weddings and other types of private events can be arranged. As a bonus, just across from the carousel and directly under the Brooklyn Bridge there is an artistic display called *The Fence in Brooklyn Bridge Park.*

To get to *Brooklyn Bridge Park* and *Jane's* Carousel, you can take the F train to York Street, walk one block up Jay Street to Front Street, turn left, walk three blocks to Main Street and turn right, which leads into the park. From the A train to High Street, or the 2 or 3 trains to Clark Street, you walk downhill on Cadman Plaza West or Henry Street, respectively, to Old Fulton Street. From Old Fulton Street, you walk 1 block and make a right on Water Street, which leads to Dock Street and into the park.

Walking Distance: DUMBO; Brooklyn Historical Society; Brooklyn Bridge; Manhattan Bridge.

JJ Hat Center

www.jjhatcenter.com

Throughout New York City, there are legions of clothes stores, small and large, where one can get various types of headwear. If you walk along the streets of *The City*, you will find souvenir stands and small cut-out establishments that also feature hats. All of these venues carry a charm to them. But if you are looking for a genuinely memorable chapeau, something for everyday use or for a special occasion, you really need to go the oldest hat store in New York City, the *JJ Hat Center*, located on 5th Avenue, just off 32nd Street.

The *JJ Hat Center* was established in 1911 and has been offering up a growing and astonishing range of hats for over a century. These days, there are over 10,000 in stock, the largest collection in *The City*. They are brought alive in a relatively small shop which features wall-to-wall hats. Display cases offer waves of styles: cloth hats, knit caps, fur hats, rain hats, caps for travel and formal hats. It goes on and on. Old-time styles are what particularly impressed me. You can get a top hat, a derby or a classic straw boater, seemingly right out of the 1920's, in this almost preposterous hat emporium.

If you are a true hat aficionado, you will find brand names from all over, from Akubra, Borsalino, Bailey of Hollywood, Monterrey, Stefeno and Hanna of Ireland, among others. Stetson, the maker of classic cowboy hats of all types, even installed a large sign out front to signify their New York partnership with the *JJ Hat Center*. The *JJ Hat Center* website alone is a great place to shop, to see images of all the different hats they carry and will ship to you, if you can't drop by 32nd Street.

A wonderful feature of the *JJ Hat Center* is the in-store *JJ Hat Workshop*, where hats are shaped, sized, crafted and repaired by the engaging staff, all of whom (naturally) wear hats that seem to fit each of them almost perfectly. This makes the experience of going to the *Center* that much better. Even if you don't wear hats, just dropping by this unique and inspired shop will bring a smile to your face and you will be compelled to try on a few if not many hats. I went there looking for a hat to wear on the occasion of my retirement from New York City transit and a Laurel & Hardy-inspired derby did the trick for me.

The F, N, R, Q trains to 34th Street Herald Square drop you off a block from the *JJ Hat Center*. The M1, M2, M3, M4 and crosstown M34 buses all stop right nearby.

Walking Distance: Empire State Building; Madison Square Garden; Flatiron Building; Mo Math; Bryant Park; New York Public Library; Irish Repertory Theatre.

John T. Brush Stairway

https://www.nycgovparks.org/parks/highbridge-park/monuments/184

While walking through *The City*, one will constantly encounter streets, avenues, parks, schools and playgrounds named after different people. Occasionally, you may even touch base with a place named after someone who you are familiar with, though did not know had a lasting memorial. A most interesting site for me as a baseball historian of sorts is the *John T. Brush Stairway*, located in Highbridge Park in Upper Manhattan, on a far-off memory of a place called Coogan's Bluff.

John Tomlinson Brush was a Civil War veteran frim Clintonville, New York who ran a few clothes stores in his home state, before moving to Indianapolis and opening a department store. To help promote the store, he got involved with baseball. In time, he would own the Indianapolis Hoosiers and the Cincinnati Reds. But he is mainly known for the third Major League team that he was associated with, the New York Giants, with whom he became the majority owner in 1902. The American League began play in 1903 and the acrimony between the two Major Leagues in those early days of the 20th Century was palpable. John T. Brush was a most vocal and key figure in all that went on between the leagues during that first decade of intense rivalry. In 1904, in what would have been the second ever modern World Series, Brush refused to pit his National League Champion Giants against the American League Champion Boston Pilgrims, on the basis that the American League was not on a talent level with the National League.

In 1905, when the Giants again won the N.L. Pennant, Brush this time agreed to a World Series match-up, but he took it a step further. He was instrumental in creating the rules which would govern the World Series, which are still used today. Brush was also a very sickly man, a victim of rheumatism and ataxia. In 1913, a year after he passed away, the Giants dedicated a stairway which led from Coogan's Bluff, a raised hill above the Giants' home, the Polo Grounds, to the ballpark below it. The stairway was refurbished in 2014 and today it is a final reminder of where a great ballpark once stood, with a headstrong owner at the helm.

To get to the *John T. Brush Stairway,* take the 1 train to 157th Street, turn right on 158th Street and Broadway and walk three blocks to Highbridge Park. The stairway is to the right. Or take the C train to 155th Street, walk a block to Edgecombe Avenue and turn left along Highbridge Park. The M2 (Edgecombe Avenue), M3 and M101 buses (Amsterdam Avenue) to 158th Street all leave you within walking distance.

Walking Distance: Highbridge Park; Morris-Jumel Mansion; Wright Brothers Playground; Hispanic Society Museum and Library; Church of the Intercession; Dance Theatre of Harlem.

Kew Gardens/Cobble Hill Cinemas

http://www.kewgardenstheatre.com/index
http://www.cobblehilltheatre.com

The advent of multiplex cinemas and the decline of grand single-screen movie houses, which began in the 1970's, signaled a loss that could never be truly quantified and/or qualified. Today, finding a first-run movie theater with even a feel for old movie houses is about as rare as finding another lost jewel, the drive-in theater. However, in New York City, there are two mirroring venues, under the same management, which do harken back to another day, even while perpetuating the economical need to live on as a multiplex. Both the *Kew Gardens Cinemas* in Queens and the *Cobble Hill Cinemas* in Brooklyn offer up not only fine and eclectic movie choices, but also a moment or two through a pocket in time, where the stars were big and the popcorn somehow tasted better.

The *Kew Gardens Cinemas* opened in the 1930's as the Austin Theater and has served the folks in Kew Gardens in a vast variety of ways. It was a double feature house for years, before being taken over by the Rugoff Theaters in the late 1950's. During the 60's art films were played there and later, United Artists purchased the theater and specialized in Midnight movies. When UA sold out, the theater became a highly successful XXX theater, until it was closed down by *The City*. The current owners bought it and restored it to its Art Deco roots and today its 6 screens include 2 upstairs where the loge and restroom areas used to be and the number 1 screen on the main floor, which includes the original mini-stage and arch. The atmosphere is created by old movie posters and Life Magazine covers that line the walls and the lone staircase. Independent and art movies are interspersed with a few mainstream flicks.

The *Cobble Hill Cinemas* at 265 Court Street was originally the Rio Theatre, which was also a double feature neighborhood house for years. It opened and closed a few times, playing first run movies and kung fu and action flicks, during various rebirths. The interior was redone and it expanded into a duplex, then a triplex; it now has 5 screens on the premises. As with *Kew Gardens*, there are old movie posters lining the walls and staircases. *Cobble Hill* also has classic scene murals on the windows above the outside marquee. These two cinema houses are unique unto themselves and really fun places to see a movie.

The E or F trains to Kew Gardens/Union Turnpike leave you with a short walk to the *Kew Gardens Cinemas*. The F or the G trains to Bergen Street leave you a few blocks from the *Cobble Hill Cinemas*.

Walking Distance: Kew Gardens: Maple Grove Park; Queens Borough Hall. Cobble Hill: New York Transit Museum; Brooklyn Borough Hall; Jackie Robinson plaque on Court & Montague Streets; Brooklyn Excelciors boarding house at 133 Clinton Street; Brooklyn Historical Society Museum.

Lincoln Center

www.lincolncenter.org

One of the most famous and far-ranging cultural centers in New York and the world itself, the *Lincoln Center for the Performing Arts* is a virtual whirlwind of activities on a daily basis and a visit to one of its 30 indoor or outdoor facilities offers the visitor a personal and unique experience, even as it touches all those around you in the same indescribable way.

In the late 1950's, a group of civic leaders, led by John D. Rockefeller III, built *Lincoln Center.* Rockefeller was credited with raising more than half of the $184.5 million dollars in private funds that helped hire various architects to build not only the iconic buildings that form the heart of Lincoln Center, but also the connected member sites. The *David Geffen Hall*, located on the North side of the main square (on Columbus Avenue, between 62nd and 65th streets) and previously known as the *Philharmonic Hall* (1962-1973) and the *Avery Fisher Hall* (1973-2015), is the home of the New York Philharmonic orchestra. The *David H. Koch Theater*, on the South side of the main square and formerly known as the *New York State Theater*, has been the home of the New York City Ballet since it first opened in 1964. And at the center of the square, between the *Koch* and the *Geffen*, sits the *Metropolitan Opera House*, or *The Met*, which opened in 1966 as a replacement for the old *Met,* which had been on Broadway and 39th street since 1883. This current home of the *Metropolitan Opera* has also seen concerts from artists beyond the opera landscape, such as The Who, Barbara Streisand and Robin Williams, a former student of the *Juilliard School,* another *Lincoln Center* building, which is located across the street from the main plaza and houses a chamber music venue, *Alice Tully Hall.*

Other popular venues in *Lincoln Center* include the *Film Society at Lincoln Center* and the *Lincoln Center Theater* on 65th Street, which features Broadway productions at the *Vivian Beaumont Theater* and off-Broadway shows at the *Mitzi E. Newhouse Theater.* Maybe the most revered site, *Jazz at Lincoln Center*, is located in the Time Warner Center on 60th Street and Broadway. There are festivals, family programs and other creative ventures on the docket at *Lincoln Center* all year long and a dedicated look at their website will surely offer up some upcoming event that can be appreciated by a particular part of the population.

The M5, M7, M10, M11, M66 and M104 bus lines all stop within one block of the *Lincoln Center for the Performing Arts.* The *66th Street/Lincoln Center* stop on the 1 train leaves you in the heart of *Lincoln Center.*

Walking Distance: American Folk Art Museum; Columbus Circle; Museum of Arts & Design; Central Park West; Time Warner Center; Carnegie Hall; City Center.

Madame Tussaud's/Ripley's Believe it or Not! Times Square

https://www.madametussauds.com/newyork
http://www.ripleysnewyork.com

As the area in and around Times Square evolved in the past few decades into a very tourist friendly site, a pair of truly enjoyable museums arrived on the scene. For New Yorkers and visitors alike, both *Madame Tussaud's Wax Museum* and the *Ripley's Believe it or Not! Odditorium* provide many laughs and a bit of wonder. The two venues, located right next to each other on 42nd Street, just off 8th Avenue, are generally crowded and waiting for even more folks to cross thorough their unique and bizarre halls.

Under the guidance of her mentor, Dr. Phillippe Curtius, Marie Tussaud (1760-1850) learned how to model wax likenesses as far back as 1777. She became the art tutor to King Louis XVI's sister at the Palace of Versailles and was commissioned during the French Revolution to make death masks of executed aristocrats. Tussaud came to Britain in the early 19th century, alongside a travelling exhibition of revolutionary relics and images of public heroes and rogues and in 1835, set up a permanent base in London. In 1883, *Madame Tussaud's Wax Museum* moved to Marylebone Road, where it remains to this day. She died in 1850, but three generations of her family kept the museum alive. *Madame Tussaud's* eventually opened branches all over the world, in places like Amsterdam, Bangkok and Sydney. Las Vegas was the first American venue chosen and in 2000, *Madame Tussaud's* in Times Square opened to great fanfare. Now a great attraction in *The City*, *Madame Tussaud's* saw another famous legacy land right next door a few years later.

Robert Ripley (1890-1949) was a cartoonist, entrepreneur and world traveler who became famous for incorporating his cartoons from the New York Globe and New York Post into a format of odd firsts, mosts and miscellaneous facts from around the world. His "*Ripley's Believe it or Not!*" franchise spanned newspapers, radio, short films and television. He opened his first museum, called "*Ripley's Believe it or Not! Odditorium*," in 1931 in Chicago. He would add museums in Dallas, Cleveland, New York, San Diego and San Francisco, before his death in 1949. New *Odditoriums* would go up throughout the world in the ensuing decades. In July 2007, *Ripley's Believe It or Not! Times Square* opened; it is the largest Ripley's museum attraction in North America, featuring a collection of over 500 unusual artifacts from all over the world.

The A, C and E trains to 42nd Street/Port Authority and the 1, 2, 3, N, Q, R and S trains to 42nd Street/Times Square all leave you a half block from *Madame Tussaud's Wax Museum* and the *Ripley's Believe it or Not! Odditorium.*

Walking Distance: B.B. King's; Port Authority Bus Terminal; Signature Theatre Company; New Victory Theater; Circle Line; Intrepid Sea, Air & Space Museum; Broadway Theater District; The Town Hall; Bryant Park; New York Public Library; Grand Central Terminal; Carolines on Broadway; Amy's Bread; Gulliver's Gate.

Marx Brothers Place & Playground

https://savemarxbrothersplace.wordpress.com

Some famous New Yorkers have their previous homes either landmarked, turned into a museum or noted by a plaque outside the property. Sometimes a person's birthplace is cited, as in the case of Theodore Roosevelt, while other times famous people who lived in New York City at the end of their lives have the residence of their final years noted, such as Mark Twain (plaque) or Edgar Allen Poe (cottage museum). The home of one set of famous New Yorkers, however, has, to date, neither landmark status nor even a plaque on the front of the building to alert all passersby that once, some future comic geniuses roamed these halls. The building at 179 East 93rd Street, in what is now called the Carnegie Hill District, was the home of the Marx Brothers, Groucho (Julius), Harpo (Adolph/Arthur), Chico (Leonard), Gummo (Milton) and Zeppo (Herbert), from around 1895 to 1909. Back then, it was called Yorkville. Today, the *93rd Street Beautification Association* has unofficially named the block between Lexington and Third Avenues, where the Marxes' old haunt stands, *Marx Brothers' Place*.

At different times, up to ten people occupied the fourth floor residence of Sam and Minnie Marx, the boys' parents. From the manic streets of Yorkville, the Marx Brothers' unique brand of total chaos comedy received its roots. For a fan of the iconic comedy team, walking by number 179 on East 93rd Street, sitting on the stoop or looking up to the fourth floor windows which once held the cacophonous wail of stage mother Minnie's future stars, is rather invigorating. But right across the street, where a recently built condominium stands, the fear of what might be looms. Without landmark status, the Marx Brothers' old home is in constant danger of a takeover by real estate speculators with no sense or care for history. The *93rd Street Beautification Association* continues to push toward saving number 179, as well as the ones around it, as landmark structures of early 20th Century Yorkville and of the famous family that once called it home.

A few blocks from *Marx Brothers Place*, at 96th Street and Second Avenue, a Parks Department sign on the front of a small park says it all: *Marx Brothers Playground.* The activity and noise one can find there is certainly a fair tribute to the spirit of the Marx Brothers, stars of vaudeville, movies, radio & television. Hopefully, a sign of even more significance can soon be put up on the wall at 179 East 93rd Street.

The 6 train to 96th Street leaves you just a few blocks from *Marx Brothers Place.* The new 96th Street stop of the Second Avenue Subway (Q train) is right next to the *Marx Brothers Playground.*

Walking Distance: Cooper Hewitt; Jewish Museum; National Academy; Solomon R. Guggenheim Museum; Central Park East; 92nd Street Y.

New York Public Library- Main Branch

http://www.nypl.org

Known as one of the finest libraries in the world, the Main Branch of the *New York Public Library (NYPL)* remains to this day one of the most recognizable buildings in the City of New York. With its pair of guardian lions, known as "*Patience*" and "*Fortitude*" since the days of transcendent Mayor Fiorello LaGuardia, sitting in omnipotence out front, the Main Branch of the *New York Public Library* offers so much to all those who are fortunate enough to pass through its halls. And though the *NYPL* does have two other expansive reference libraries, The *Schomburg Center for Research in Black Studies* at 135th Street and Lenox Avenue and the *New York Public Library for the Performing Arts* at Lincoln Center, the Main Branch is the one that is singularly thought of by the public at large as THE *New York Public Library.*

Located on 5th Avenue between 40th and 42nd Streets, the Main Branch of the *New York Public Library* opened in May of 1911, with President William Howard Taft, Governor John Alden Dix and Mayor William Jay Gaynor in attendance. Even as continuing changes in Bryant Park at the rear of the *NYPL* were going on, the now familiar stone and Vermont marble entrance gave the earliest visitors a most proper feel for the impressive halls within.

The *NYPL's* most celebrated Rose Main Reading Room (Room 315) has thousands of reference volumes on its perimeter and features 16 ft. high ceilings, huge windows, chandeliers, long wooden tables and brass lamps. These days, there are also computers with Internet access and ports for laptop usage; library workers will efficiently bring requested material to all those who happen by, be you a scholar on a project or an everyday New Yorker merely trying to enhance your knowledge base. For research or reading purposes, the *NYPL* is second to none. Audio books, musical recordings, photo collections, and video of all types are in the offing. In addition, there are always traveling exhibits on display, generally on the main floor.

For decades, Norbert Pearlroth, Robert Ripley's main researcher, spent 10 hours a day here, for 6 days a week, finding items to be used on *Ripley's Believe it or Not!* In 1965, the NYPL was designated a National Historic Landmark and in 1966 it was added to the National Register of Historic Places.

The B, D, F and M trains to 42nd Street/Bryant Park leave you a block from the entrance to the *NYPL*. In addition, all trains that go to Grand Central Terminal, 5th Avenue/42nd Street or Times Square/42nd Street leave you just a short walk from the Main Branch of the *New York Public Library.*

Walking Distance: The Morgan Library & Museum; Bryant Park; The Town Hall; Grand Central Terminal; B.B. King's; Madame Tussaud's Wax Museum; Ripley's Believe It or Not Odditorium; New Victory Theater; Broadway Theater District; Port Authority Bus Terminal; Intrepid Sea, Air & Space Museum; St. Patrick's Cathedral; United Nations; Amy's Bread; Gulliver's Gate.

New Victory Theater

http://www.newvictory.org

Bringing the arts to young people is an item that really should be addressed, whenever possible. The need for a theater or live performance experience that caters to kids is something that can be so far reaching to their future, that we as a society should embrace it. Enter the *New Victory Theater* in Times Square, a most innovative and imaginative venue. In the *New Victory Theater*, the whole experience of going to live theater is offered up for children, while also serving as a great respite for the adults who choose to take their young kids or grandchildren to this most delightful site.

The history of the building that has housed the current *New Victory Theater* since 1995 is fascinating. It was built in 1900 by Oscar Hammerstein, the grandfather of the legendary Broadway lyricist of the same name. Then called the *Theatre Republic*, it remained a viable Broadway theater for decades, before being turned into Broadway's first burlesque club in the 1930's by a legend of that genre, Billy Minsky. In 1942, in deference to the United States' World War II effort, the theater was renamed the *Victory* and played first run movies for a few decades. By 1972, Times Square had become a more adult-oriented and decadent area and the *Victory* became the Big Street's only XXX-rated movie theater. The *New 42nd Street* group, which cleaned up a number of beaten down theaters in the area in the 1990's, spawned the current *New Victory Theater*, which caters to children and families. In many ways, this transformation is the greatest example of what Times Square was and has become.

The theater itself is small and intimate, with mezzanine and balcony levels that are in close enough proximity for kids to see all the fabulous technology-driven shows that play at the *New Victory*. Beyond the theater, all arts are in the mix, as dance, music and circus acts all make the *New Victory Theater* a leading family entertainment facility. Sitting in the balcony for a vibrant production of the Jules Verne classic "*20,000 Leagues Under the Sea*," I overheard an exchange between an 8-year old and his uncle. The young boy asked if the building was going to be "retired" or closed down any time soon. When the uncle asked what his nephew meant, the kid replied in a decidedly pointed way. "I hope they don't retire this place, because I want to come back here." Now that's a most relevant endorsement.

The A, C and E trains to 42nd Street/Port Authority and the 1, 2, 3, N, Q, R and S trains to 42nd Street/Times Square all leave you within a half block of the *New Victory Theater*.

Walking Distance: B.B. King's; Madame Tussaud's Wax Museum; Ripley's Believe It or Not Odditorium; Port Authority Bus Terminal; Circle Line; Intrepid Sea, Air & Space Museum; Signature Theatre Company; Broadway Theater District; Bryant Park; The Town Hall; New York Public Library; Grand Central Terminal; Amy's Bread; Gulliver's Gate.

Old Town Bar & Restaurant

http://www.oldtownbar.com

Over the years, many of the cozy local watering holes that once smattered across the New York City landscape have slowly disappeared, mostly due to the emergence of newer clubs and/or changing neighborhoods. But there are still some classic Irish pubs around which last dominated the scene in the 1970's and 1980's. A particular venue which has held firm for over a century can be found right in the midst of the thriving Flatiron District. The *Old Town Bar & Restaurant*, located on 18th Street, just off Broadway, is a jewel from another time.

When the *Old Town Bar & Restaurant* opened in 1892, it was called *Viemeisters* and served a German menu for many years. During Prohibition, now called *Craig's Restaurant*, the *Old Town* operated as a Tammany Hall speakeasy. Booths were built with secret hiding places for liquor bottles, which are still there today. After Prohibition, the *Old Town* adopted the name it still uses. Inside, you will find almost all of the original accoutrements. The 55-foot mahogany and marble bar and the 16-foot high tin ceilings are original, while the huge urinals in the Men's Room were installed in 1910. The dumbwaiters at the end of the bar, which now carry food and drink up and down between the bar and the kitchen and dining room on the second floor, are the oldest such active restaurant conveyers in *The City.*

These days, the *Old Town* continues to be a great place for folks to get together for a beer or a bite after work, if only to talk and soak in the atmosphere of a place that maintains a laid back, dusky feel. They say the *Old Town* is in "*eternal twilight.*" There are various brands of beer on tap and to eat, you can get basic pub food, burgers, sandwiches, salads and small appetizers. A wall near the front entrance features books autographed by Irish authors like Frank

McCourt, Jim Dwyer and poet Seamus Heaney. From 1983-92, the *Old Town* appeared in the opening credits of NBC'S "*Late Night with David Letterman*" and movies like "*State of Grace*," "*The Devil's Own*" and "*Bullets over Broadway*" also had scenes shot there, but it has never been run like a celebrity bar. Still, there are many photos on the walls of famous people who have quietly passed on through this most comfortable pub. The dining room upstairs, a great place for small groups to escape the hum of the bar below, can be rented out for parties. '

The L, N, Q, R, 4, 5 and 6 trains to Union Square/East 14th Street all leave you a short walk from the *Old Town Bar & Restaurant*.

Walking Distance: Union Square Park, Theodore Roosevelt Birthplace; Flatiron Building; Irish Repertory Theatre; Museum of Mathematics; Washington Square Park.

One World Observatory at One World Trade Center

https://oneworldobservatory.com

The first thing I wanted to know was what would it be called? As it was being built, it was referred to as the Freedom Tower or the new World Trade Center, but ultimately the new high rise in Downtown Manhattan became *One World Trade Center.* Located right in the shadow of the original World Trade Center, which is now, of course, the *9/11 Memorial* and the *9/11 Museum*, the sightseeing deck, *One World Observatory at One World Trade Center,* is a nice addition to the history of New York skyscrapers.

Following the terrorist attacks of September 11, 2001, one of the questions that circled around was whether a new high rise building should be built where the fallen Twin Towers once stood. Some felt that it served no tangible purpose, while others believed that constructing a new World Trade Center, one or two buildings, was essential, to honor the original ones and/or to give notice to the terrorists that we would not live in fear. It took a while, but after a proper memorial on the footprint of the Twin Towers and an adjacent museum both finally became a reality, a single tall building, dubbed *One World Trade Center* went up, just to the North of the sacred space called *Ground Zero.* In 2015, *One World Observatory,* the viewing wing of *One World Trade Center*, opened to its first visitors.

One World Observatory has all the feel that a high rise perch built in the 21st Century should, in that the creators have taken the use of technology to a requisite level. Before you even reach the 100th floor, where you can experience a 360-degree vantage point, covering New York and New Jersey, you are primed with a brief video downstairs and an interactive look at *The City* all around you as you go up the elevator. Once you get to the observation deck, you are offered a computer tablet, which serves as an audio tour, available in several languages, to walk you around the sites you see below. The tablet looks very cool but it requires an extra fee, which seemed like double dipping to me. There is also an interactive presentation delivered by an employee on the southern wing of the observatory. Ultimately though, it is the act of looking down on sites like the Brooklyn Bridge, the Statue of Liberty and the Empire State Building that makes this a great place to visit.

The A, C, J, Z, 2, 3, 4 and 5 trains to Fulton Street leave you a few blocks from *One World Observatory*. The R and W trains to Cortlandt Street are also just a few blocks away.

Walking Distance: Museum of American Finance; South Street Seaport District; Pier 6 Helicopter Tours; 9/11 Memorial & Museum; Federal Hall; Skyscraper Museum; Museum of Jewish Heritage; National Museum of the American Indian; Battery Park; Irish Hunger Memorial; Canyon of Heroes; Statue of Liberty/Ellis Island Ferries; Staten Island Ferry.

Prospect Park Zoo & Lefferts Historic House Museum

http://prospectparkzoo.com
https://www.prospectpark.org/visit-the-park/places-to-go/lefferts-historic-house

Two very enjoyable sites are located just a few hundred yards from one another in Brooklyn's fabulous Prospect Park. Both the *Prospect Park Zoo* and the *Lefferts Historic House Museum* can bring a smile to a child of any age.

The *Prospect Park Zoo* opened in 1935, as part of a city playground, park and zoo renovation project. It operated for 53 years under the Department of Parks and Recreation, before being closed for 5 years, due to renovations. Since re-opening in 1993, it has provided Brooklynites with a great venue to bring their children, right in the midst of the borough's signature park Children's educational programs are offered and they're deeply involved in the restoration of endangered species. A few peacocks walk freely around the main fairways, which is an endearing sight. All in all, the *Prospect Park Zoo* is a solid member of the New York City zoo community.

Just down the block from the zoo sits the *Lefferts Historic House Museum.* Built by Pieter Lefferts in 1783, it is another of the few surviving farmhouses in *The City.* Lefferts, a lieutenant in the Continental Army during the Revolutionary War, was later a Kings County judge. Today, his preserved home, featuring period piece furniture, serves as an example of life in Brooklyn in the early 1800's. With a yard out front and the Prospect Park carousel directly across from it, the *Lefferts House* is particularly fine place for children's birthday parties. The *Prospect Park Zoo* is also available for kids' parties.

The eastern side of Prospect Park is a wonderful area to spend time with family and friends. Besides the *Prospect Park Zoo*, the *Lefferts Historic House Museum* and the carousel, the Brooklyn Botanic Garden is right across the street from all three venues. To the south of the park is the Prospect Park Boathouse & Audubon Center. And if you are a baseball historian, the Prospect Park Parade Ground, once the storied home of Brooklyn amateur baseball and now featuring restored baseball, football, tennis and soccer fields, is at the southern tip of the park, while the former site of Ebbets Field, now an apartment complex, is just a few blocks away from the eastern side. Overall, Prospect Park remains one of the great parks in *The City*

The B and Q trains and the local S shuttle to the Prospect Park station leave you right down the block from the *Lefferts Historic House Museum* and the *Prospect Park Zoo.* The B41 bus stops in front of the zoo and the B47 bus to Flatbush Avenue and Empire Boulevard leaves you just down the street.

Walking Distance: Brooklyn Botanic Garden; Brooklyn Museum; Prospect Park Carousel; Prospect Park Parade Ground; Ebbets Field Apartments (former site of Ebbets Field).

Queens Zoo

http://queenszoo.com

Much like *Central Park*, a larger and more universally known area, *Flushing Meadows/Corona Park* is a wonderful place to spend a day, in so many ways. And the *Queens Zoo*, located at 53-51 111th Street, is another of the great venues within the most vibrant park in Queens.

The circular trail that takes you through the main artery of the *Queens Zoo* is almost soothing, particularly in the early morning. The various animals in the zoo are spread out in a calculated way, to give one a chance to take each one in; from alligators to coyotes to lynx, each cut-out area has a singular charm. And in the *Queens Zoo*, you can get as close a look at a bison as one can find. Having seen bison running free in Yellowstone Park, which was very exciting, the sight of the tranquil Bison in the *Queens Zoo* gave me some perspective, as to the actual size and temperament of these animals.

Like many zoos, a big attraction is the sea lion pool. In the case of the *Queens Zoo*, the sea lion pool is not that big and there are only a few sea lions on site, so when one of the three daily feedings comes up, you really have a close-up look at them. The sea lions here come out of the water almost boldly, going up onto the enclosed land area, where the feeders oblige them, pretty much face-to-face. Across from the sea lion pool is the *Sea Lion Store and Café*, a great place to take a breath while stopping for a bite or buying a souvenir.

The *Queens Zoo's* dedication to conservancy is noted throughout the zoo, with different interactive areas for young and old alike to consider the welfare of wildlife. A most interesting spot for me was the *Extinct Species Graveyard*, where animals that have become extinct (some for centuries) are memorialized. The *Aviary* inside the zoo is modest, yet as noisy as any of the larger ones that I have been to. (It seems they got the loudest group of birds that were available.) The petting zoo features goats, horses, longhorn steer and a huge hog. There is also a learning center in the petting zoo and just across from the petting zoo is a great children's carousel. Overall, the *Queens Zoo* is a superb young children's zoo.

If you take the 7 train to 111th Street, it's about a 5-minute walk down 111th street to the *Queens Zoo*. If you take the Q58 bus to Corona Avenue and walk east to 111th St., the pedestrian walkway on your left leads to the *Queens Zoo.*

Walking Distance: Queens Museum; Hall of Science; U.S. Tennis Center; Tavern on the Green; Lemon Ice King of Corona; Citi Field; Louis Armstrong House Museum.

St. George Theatre

https://www.stgeorgetheatre.com

Constructed in the same Era as the Loew's Wonder Theatres, the *St. George Theatre* in Staten Island is another classic old hall that has been brought alive through some renovations done by very generous individuals. Located at 35 Hyatt Street, a short walk from the ferry terminal, the *St. George Theatre* was once considered the most magnificent theatre in the borough. And since its revival in the early 21st Century, it may well be again.

Solomon Brill of the Isle Theatrical Company, was an independent owner of 15 theatres in the New York City area at a time when most movie houses were built by Hollywood studios. He began construction in 1928 and the *St. George* opened its doors on December 4th, 1929 as a movie and vaudeville house, where one could see a flick and catch a live performance in the same sitting. This two-tiered entertainment was abandoned in 1934, but revived during the 1940's to help sell war bonds. After World War II, it remained a movie palace until 1977, under the stewardship of the Fabian Theater chain, which had acquired the *St. George* in 1938.

Subsequent owners used the venue for a roller rink, an antique showroom and a night club, all unsuccessful ventures. In the mid-1990's, it briefly opened as a performing arts center, but closed down quickly. The *St. George Theatre* remained silent until 2003, when the film "*School of Rock*" used it for its final scene. In 2004, Mrs. Rosemary Cappozalo and her daughters, Luanne Sorrentino and Doreen Cugno, started a not-for-profit organization to save this historic theatre from being torn down with Cappozalo donating over a million dollars for a renovation of the site. Since re-opening in June of 2004, over 800 events have been held there, with performers like Tony Bennett, Jerry Seinfeld, Whoopi Goldberg and Pat Benatar & Neil Giraldo among the headliners.

Today, the *St. George Theatre*, which originally held 2,800 people, seats 1,700, with plans to expand in the near future. It is a fine place to see a show of any kind, with the distinctive look of the old, classic movie palaces of the 1930's, including murals on the walls in the lobby, winding staircases to the mezzanine and stained-glass chandeliers. The updated sound system is another attractive reason to drop by to see a show at this wonderful venue.

The 1 train to South Ferry, the 4 and 5 to Bowling Green and the R and W to Whitehall Street/South Ferry all leave you by the Manhattan entrance to the Staten Island Ferry. Upon arrival at the St. George Ferry Terminal in Staten Island, the *St. George Theatre* is two blocks away, at 35 Hyatt Street.

Walking Distance: Staten Island Museum (St. George branch); Richmond County Bank Ballpark; St. George Ferry Terminal; National Lighthouse Museum.

St. Patrick's Cathedral

http://www.saintpatrickscathedral.org

Probably the most famous church or place of worship in New York City, *St. Patrick's Cathedral* remains today a must-see venue for both tourists and wandering New Yorkers. *St. Patrick's* was the brainchild of Bishop John Hughes, the first archbishop in New York (1850), who announced in 1853 that the Catholic church planned "*to erect a Cathedral in the City of New York that may be worthy of our increasing numbers, intelligence and wealth as a religious community, and at all events, worthy, as a public architectural monument, of the present and prospective crowns of this metropolis of the American continent.*" This new cathedral was slated to improve on the original *St. Patrick's Cathedral*, which had stood on Mulberry Street since 1815. (The old *St. Pat's* burned down in 1866, but was rededicated on St. Patrick's Day in 1868. Today, it is oldest Catholic church in New York City).

On August 15, 1858, the cornerstone was laid for the new *St. Patrick's Cathedral*, located on Fifth Avenue, between 50th and 51st Streets. In 1864, following the death of Archbishop Hughes, Bishop John McCloskey was named the new archbishop of New York. The new cathedral, whose construction was interrupted by the Civil War, resumed when the war ended. In 1875, Archbishop McCloskey is installed at the first American Cardinal and on May 25, 1879, the new *St. Patrick's* opens under his stewardship, to great fanfare. In 1888, the famous spires of the cathedral were completed, under the guidance of Archbishop Michael Corrigan. *St. Patrick's Cathedral* would become the unofficial starting point for the St. Patrick's Day Parade and as such, March 17th might still be the best time to drop by, amongst the festive New York crowd.

The interior was restored in 1972 under Cardinal Cooke and a restoration of the exterior was completed in time for the 100th

anniversary ceremony in 1979. Television monitors were added inside the cathedral under Cardinal O'Connor (1984-2000) and with Cardinal Egan (2000-2009) presiding, Pope Benedict XVI became the first Pope to say mass at *St. Patrick's* on April 19, 2008. A two-year steam cleaning of the cathedral's front entrance was completed in late 2014, while renovations within were again made from May of 2015 to July of 2016. Even when the scaffolding was inside, *St. Patrick's Cathedral* remained a wonderful place to briefly rest, light a candle, say a prayer or just take in the classic architecture.

The B, D, F and M trains to the *47th -50th Street/Rockefeller Center* stop and the N, Q and R trains on the *49th Street* stop all leave you just a few blocks from *St. Patrick's Cathedral.* The M1, M2, M3 buses on Madison and Fifth Avenues have stops near the cathedral.

Walking Distance: Rockefeller Center; Radio City Music Hall; The Town Hall; B.B. King's; Madame Tussaud's Wax Museum; Ripley's Believe It or Not Odditorium; New Victory Theater; Grand Central Terminal; Bryant Park; New York Public Library-Main Branch; Gulliver's Gate.

Signature Theatre Company

http://www.signaturetheatre.org/index.aspx

The *Signature Theatre* or the *Pershing Square Signature Center*, its official name, is a most unique venue, where the work of playwrights is delved into in a concrete manner. A regional theatre company located at 480 West 42nd Street (between 9th and 10th Avenues), the *Signature Theatre* has consistently put on numerous top notch productions each year, for over a quarter of a century.

Founded in 1991 by James Houghton, the *Signature Theatre Company* was the first regional company to devote an entire season to the works of a single playwright. Their mission is clearly stated on their website; *"Signature Theatre Company exists to honor and celebrate the playwright."* There are three residencies that make up the *Signature Theatre Company. Residency One*, Signature's one-year residency, explores a series of plays from the body of work of one writer. *Residency Five*, a new, five-year residency, offers three full productions of premiere plays to a group of writers. And the *Legacy Program*, which is described as a homecoming for past Signature Playwrights-in-Residence, in the form of a production of a premiere or *Signature* play.

The best part of the *Signature Theatre*, to this supporter of their programs, is the intimacy of the three small theatres that make up the *Pershing Square Signature Center.* The 294-seat Irene Diamond Theatre is, in and of itself, an embracing setting, but the Alice Griffin Jewel Box Theatre and the Romulus Linney Courtyard Theatre, which each hold just 191 people, offer up unique takes on the intricacies of on-stage performance. The idea (first articulated about The Town Hall) that "there is not a bad seat in the house," something no Broadway theatre can seriously claim, is a living, breathing reality in the three micro-theatres that make up the *Signature Center.* On site, there is also a café and a bookstore, as well as the Ford Foundation Studio

Theatre, a state-of-the-art performance and rehearsal space where *Signature* artists share their latest work or develop their upcoming production.

In 2016, the *Signature Theatre Company* celebrated its 25th season with a number of diverse pieces from various playwrights and performers. From the latest re-make of Sam Shepard's 1979 ground breaking *Buried Child,* starring veteran stars Ed Harris and Amy Madigan, to the manic tribute to the days of the vaudeville clown, *Old Hats*, with the amazing team of Bill Irwin and David Shiner, as well as the fabulous musical talent of Shaina Taub, the *Signature Theatre Company* continues to offer some of the best Off-Broadway entertainment that one can be a party to.

The Times Square or Port Authority stations of the 1, 2, 3, A, C, E, N, Q and R trains all leave you a few blocks from the *Pershing Square Signature Center.* The M11 bus also stops right near the *Center.*

Walking Distance: Port Authority Bus Terminal; Circle Line; Intrepid Sea, Air & Space Museum; Broadway Theater District; B.B. King's; Madame Toussaud's Wax Museum; Ripley's Believe it or Not Odditorium; Bryant Park; New York Public Library; Grand Central Terminal; Amy's Bread; Gulliver's Gate.

S'Mac

www.smacnyc.com

Word of mouth will lead you to various types of eating establishments, with your own personal preferences or sense of adventure guiding you. One great type of place to dine is the single-theme venue, one which makes different types of foods, based on one central item. Burgers, chicken, hot dogs and fish have all inspired both fast food and singularly owned restaurants. Soup joints rose up in the 80's and 90's with a famous sitcom upping the already impressive volume of one stop in Midtown. But of all of them, the idea of a shop that sells only macaroni and cheese piqued my fancy. There have been a few, but *S'Mac* is a must try, if I am any judge.

Ironically enough, Sarita and Caesar Ekya got the idea for a macaroni and cheese specialty shop while they were eating at *Peanut Butter & Company*, a since closed peanut butter and jelly spot near Washington Square Park. In June of 2006, the Ekya's opened for business, serving ten different varieties of macaroni and cheese. Today, from two sites in *The City*, they work off a menu of 12 varieties, while constantly adding new types of mac-n-cheese to their repertoire. Located in the East Village at 345 East 12th Street, between 1st and 2nd avenues and in Murray Hill, at 157 East 33rd Street, between Lexington and 3rd Avenues, *S'Mac* (short for *Sarita's Mac and Cheese*) is a great place to grab a quick bite, a hearty lunch or fuel a full blown party of macaroni and cheese lovers.

There are four sizes that one can order, with very pointed names: *Nosh, Major Munch, Mongo* and *Partay*. From *Buffalo Chicken, 4-Cheese, Cheeseburger* to basic *All-American* and more, there is a mac-n-cheese for everyone. You can order multi-grain or gluten-free macaroni for an additional cost and all *S'Mac* varieties can be served with or without bread crumbs. (Go crumbs, trust me.) You can also make a special order of your own, using up to 2 cheeses and 3 mix-in items (or more, for a fee). Both shops deliver in an around their local areas, but a visit to *S'Mac* is your best choice, since there are usually new mixes being experimented with, which makes *S'Mac* even more attractive.

The L train to 14th Street and First Avenue is right near the *S'Mac* on 12th Street, as are the buses that run on First Avenue. The 6 train to Astor Place and all the lines that stop at 14th Street/Union Square leave you a short walk from there. The 6 train to 33rd Street/Park Avenue is a few blocks from the Murray Hill site and buses on Third and Lexington Avenues stop nearby.

Walking Distance: East Village: Tompkins Square Park; Museum of the American Gangster; New Museum; Basilica at Old St. Patrick's Cathedral; Washington Square Park. Murray Hill: Empire State Building; Madison Square Garden.

South Street Seaport District

http://www.southstreetseaport.com

Following Hurricane Sandy in 2012, many coastal areas faced long, uphill battles to regain their former reality. Beyond the neighborhoods in places like Staten Island or the Rockaways, where human lives were in the balance, the *South Street Seaport District*, a most historic New York area, is a venue which desperately needs to regain a hold on not just tourism, but the lifetime New Yorkers who have passed through its corridors in decades past. That revival had begun in 2014 and was gaining steam, as the year 2017 transpired.

The *South Street Seaport Museum* was chartered in the late 1960's by preservationists who deemed that a few blocks in the *South Street Seaport District* were worthy of maintaining. These early and mid-19th Century buildings, along with the adjacent piers, which housed historic ships, would help form the *South Street Seaport Museum.* Schermerhorn Row, a group of a dozen buildings designed by 1812 by Peter Schermerhorn, were a kind of novelty on the East River and the many ships that filled the harbor delivered countless imports, like cotton, molasses, coffee and tea. This trade market helped shape not only the *South Street Seaport District*, but a growing New York City itself.

Today, the lobby of 12 Fulton Street, one of the historic Schermerhorn Row buildings, is open from Wednesday through Sunday, 11 AM to 5 PM, with rotating interpretive displays and activities for all ages. Current access to the galleries there is by appointment or for education programs only. The Bowne Printers and Maritime Craft Center at 207-209 Water Street offer up examples of 19th Century craftsmanship. (Note: during the renovation period on South Street, the craft shop will not have regular operating hours, but the print workshops are open to individual or school groups.)

The *Street of Ships on Pier 16* are open to the public, highlighted by the German barque *Peking* (built in Hamburg in 1911) and the Lightship *Ambrose* (LV87), built in 1907 to guide ships safely from the Atlantic Ocean into the broad mouth of lower New York Bay, between Coney Island, New York and Sandy Hook, New Jersey. A fascinating timeline exhibit, *Seaport: Past & Future*, from the early days as a trade giant, through the heyday of the legendary (and since departed) *Fulton Fish Market*, to the emerging post-Sandy district, lines the border of Pier 17. Along Fulton Street, a string of minute food stands have been set up and there are walking tours available. A new iPic Theatre, where one can watch a movie while dining, opened in the Seaport in October of 2016.

The A, C, J, Z, 2, 3, 4 and 5 trains to Fulton Street all leave you within walking distance, down Fulton Street, of the *South Street Seaport District.*

Walking Distance: Museum of American Finance; Federal Hall; 9/11 Memorial & Museum; Pier 6 Helicopter Tours; National Museum of the American Indian; Battery Park; One World Observatory; Canyon of Heroes; Statue of Liberty/Ellis Island Ferries; Staten Island Ferry.

Strawberry Fields

http://www.centralpark.com/guide/attractions/strawberry-fields.html

There are a number of singular spots in New York City which summon the memory of an individual who lived in *The City* and graced its streets during their time of residence. One of the most symbolic of these venues is a small patch of land just inside the 72nd Street entrance to Central Park West. Named after a song that was about an orphanage which existed on the other side of the Atlantic Ocean, *Strawberry Fields* is a most significant place for both New Yorkers and visitors alike. The memory of John Lennon, one of the greatest poets of the 20th Century, is celebrated here, just a block from where the former Beatle was gunned down.

The night of December 8, 1980, when John Lennon was assassinated in the courtyard of his home, the Dakota building, the reaction worldwide was of unmitigated shock. In the months following his death, the image of Lennon, who had just released a very successful new album, *Double Fantasy*, remained a global rallying point for the abolishment of senseless violence, before it slowly faded away. But in New York, where his wife, Yoko Ono and young son, Sean, still lived, the feeling of grief was palpable for years.

On what would have been Lennon's 45th birthday, October 9, 1985, *Strawberry Fields* was dedicated in Central Park West, in the shadows of the Dakota building. A circular tile mosaic with word "*IMAGINE*" situated at its core highlighted the area which would forever be known as "*Strawberry Fields*" from that day forward and cited another of Lennon's most famous and popular songs. Since then, this "*Quiet Zone*" as a sign at its entrance notes, has become a place of pilgrimage for people from all around the world, to reflect on the prolific, short life and pointless death of a celebrated man of peace.

Strawberry Fields is New York's memorial to its fallen, adopted son, a guy who went from almost unimaginable world fame in his 20's to being just another 40-year old walking the streets of Manhattan with a cheery "*Hello*'" and a predisposition to sign the odd autograph request, on the rare occasion when he was approached at all. Today, a walk through *Strawberry Fields* has an almost spiritual feel to it and is highly recommended for anyone wishing to contemplate peace for even a moment or two.

The 1, 2 and 3 trains to the *72nd Street/Broadway Station* all leave you a few blocks from the 72nd Street entrance to Central Park. The A, B and D trains stop part time at 72nd Street, right near the entrance to the park and the M10 and M72 buses also stop near the park's entrance.

Walking Distance: Beacon Theatre; The Triad; Lincoln Center for the Performing Arts; The Folk Art Museum; Swedish Cottage Marionette Theatre; New-York Historical Society; American Museum of Natural History.

The Basilica of St. Patrick's Old Cathedral

http://oldcathedral.org

Some jewels of the *The City* hold a special place to parts of the community. St. Patrick's Cathedral on 5th Avenue, between 50th and 51st Streets has served the Catholic Church admirably since 1879. Before that grand building was erected, though, there was a smaller and more intimate place of worship, which helped guide Catholics through some stormy times. Built in the years 1809-1815, *St. Patrick's Old Cathedral,* the original, still stands in the same spot at 263 Mulberry Street, bordered by Prince, Mott and Houston Streets, on the edge of Little Italy. The cathedral was given Basilica status by Pope Benedict XVI on St. Patrick's Day, 2010, which is traditionally afforded due to a site's antiquity, dignity, architectural and artistic worth, and/or significance as a center of worship due to historical value. As such, *The Basilica of St. Patrick's Old Cathedral* provides one with a modest look back at another time and place which somehow resonates today.

The history of *St. Patrick's Old Cathedral* is ripe with both triumph and tragedy. Conflicts which turned into rioting between Irish Catholics and anti-Catholic factions in 1836 almost resulted in the destruction of the church which a fire, decades later, in 1866, succeeded in doing. The church was rebuilt in 1868, even as the new St. Patrick's was already under construction. When the original opened in 1815, the recently ordained second Bishop of New York, John Connolly, took up residence. Until 1830, the annual St. Patrick's Day Parade ended at *Old St. Pat's*, before moving its destination to the Church of the Transfiguration on Ann Street and ultimately Fifth Avenue, where it would and still does begin, near the new St. Pat's.

Following a renovation for its 200th Anniversary celebration on November 22, 2015, *The Basilica of St. Patrick's Old Cathedral,* when approached and then entered, offers up a rash of contemplation.

Squeezed into the tight streets of the neighborhood, one can imagine when the church first stood, in a much more rural setting. And since 1879, it has in fact been a neighborhood church, which suits the relatively tiny structure, when compared to its grandiose replacement uptown. Designated a New York landmark in 1966 and added to the National Register of Historic Places in 1977, *The Basilica of St. Patrick's Old Cathedral*, with underground catacombs which contain remains of bishops and early New Yorkers, will hopefully, through the efforts of the current renovations, stand tall for a few more centuries to come.

The N or the R trains to Prince Street or the 6 train to Spring Street all drop you off a few blocks from *The Basilica of St. Patrick's Old Cathedral.*

Walking Distance: New Museum; S'Mac: Ukrainian Museum; Museum at Eldridge Street; Museum of Chinese in America; The Drawing Center; The Meatball Shop; Tompkins Square Park; Lower East Side Tenement Museum.

The Cell Theatre

http://www.thecelltheatre.org

New York City is the greatest place in the world for performance art of all kinds. The Broadway theatre district constantly offers up new shows and revivals of previously performed classics or crowd favorites. The pure largesse of the Broadway stage brings with it a magic that cannot be replicated. Whether a particular show features long time stage actors, major film stars making their live debut or new and exciting talent arriving in a whirlwind, Broadway is a most unique New York thing. Off-Broadway shows, in smaller theatres and halls all around *The City* also can inspire an anxious crowd, in a more up close setting. Then there are the even smaller venues in New York City where aspiring artists of all kinds can present original works of their own, in a most intimate setting. One of the finer ones that one can encounter is *Nancy Manocherian's Cell Theatre*, located at 338 West 23rd Street, off Eighth Avenue. *The Cell* is a minute hall that seats approximately 60 people and as such, is quite conducive to poetry readings, one-man or one-woman shows, or performance art that is in its earliest stages. A visit to *The Cell Theatre* is a most refreshing stop off the main road.

Featuring 20′ ceilings, a balcony and professional lighting, sound, and projection equipment, *The Cell* is available to rent for any type of performance that might fit the venue. There are also a pair of artists' salons that call *The Cell* home. The *Blackboard Reading Series*, which is devoted to Black Playwrights takes place every 2nd Monday of the month. And the *Irish American Writers & Artists*, created by the fabulous Malachy McCourt, allows *IAW&A* members the opportunity to present a reading from a work in progress, a video, a comedy skit, personal stories or songs. Each of these groups lend a welcome texture to the charm of *The Cell.*

Among other wonderful recent works at *The Cell*, Irish poet

Connie Roberts held the launch party for her premiere book of poetry, *Little Witness*, which spoke of her rather trying childhood, in which she spent years in oft-times brutal Irish industrial schools. And John McDonagh, a New York cab driver and radio personality for over 30 years, premiered his original one-man show, *Cabtivist*, which offered a slew of hilarious tales encountered during his manic career driving others around the streets of *The City*.

The 23rd Street stops of the C, E, F, M, N, R, Q, 1 and 2 trains all leave you either right near *The Cell Theatre,* or just a few avenues away. The M23 (23rd Street), M20 (8th Avenue) and M11 (9th Avenue) buses all stop near *The Cell.*

Walking Distance: High Line; Chelsea; Whitney Museum of Art; Flatiron Building; Old Town Bar and Restaurant; Madison Square Park; Irish Repertory Theatre; The Meatball Shop.

The Lemon Ice King of Corona

http://thelemonicekingofcorona.com

A local legend in Queens, *The Lemon Ice King of Corona*, located at 52-02 108th street in, yes, Corona, Queens, is a most beloved and special stop on the way, for anyone wishing to see not only the famous sites in *The City*, but also one of the hidden jewels that have been a part of the New York landscape for generations.

Way back in the year 1944, Nicola Benfaremo opened his shop in the heart of the mostly Italian neighborhood of Corona. In total accord with the early immigrants from Italy, who made their own ices using actual pieces of fruit and natural ingredients, Benfaremo was really bringing a treasured part of the Old Country to the local masses. His little shop quickly became the pride of Corona. In time, it would be so much more.

The beauty of *The Lemon Ice King of Corona* is that they are all made on the premises. Peter Benfaremo, Nicola's son, who has been on the scene all his life, still uses cases of lemons and oranges to get true tastes into his product and, as noted, all the flavors have real fruit pieces in them. This goes for blueberry to raspberry to watermelon to banana. There are crushed peanuts in the peanut butter ice and shavings of coconut in the coconut ice. Wonderful hybrids like cherry/vanilla, orange/vanilla and strawberry/banana are singular treats, while favorites like cherry, grape, pineapple and of course, lemon, never disappoint.

The Lemon Ice King of Corona has been recognized as the gold standard for Italian ices for decades, though Peter Benfaremo prefers the term "water ices," owning up to the fact that the Italian part of the name is more about the person making them being an Italian. No matter how you look at it, *The Lemon Ice King of Corona* is a very refreshing part of the New York City scene. Not surprisingly, it has been featured in numerous magazines as a must place to visit. Sugar free ices are available and they also serve five flavors of gourmet candy apples. When coming to order from the window of the small corner shop, the only rule to know is that they will not mix flavors. Besides the usual small, medium or large cups, you can also order bulk packages (pint, quart, etc.) to go, which, along with the candy apples, can provide a great addition to a kids' party.

If you take the 7 train to 111th Street, then walk down to 108th Street and turn left, *The Lemon Ice King of Corona* is about 10 blocks up. The Q23 and the Q58 buses both stop right near the shop, as well.

Walking Distance: Queens Museum; Hall of Science; U.S. Tennis Center; Tavern on the Green; Queens Zoo; Citi Field; Louis Armstrong House Museum.

The New York Aquarium

http://nyaquarium.com

Coney Island, long a favored tourist stop, has been revitalized in the 21st Century, following the openings of the Brooklyn Cyclones' ballpark and a new Luna Park. Besides the Wonder Wheel, the Cyclone rollercoaster and Nathan's Famous, another weather-beaten site on the fringes of the area still excites and entertains as much as the more heralded attractions at Coney. *The New York Aquarium*, the oldest continually operating aquarium in the United States, opened in Castle Garden in Battery Park, Manhattan, in 1896, and has been at Coney Island since 1957. It is currently in the process of re-inventing itself, even as the familiar stop retains its former glory.

Upon entering the *New York Aquarium* these days, you encounter two indoor areas, which consist of fish from all over. The *Glover's Reef* and the *Conservation Hall* are in many ways the most important part of the park, as they set the tone for the outdoor sites that lie ahead. One only needs to stand in a corner at either of these halls and watch the absolute joy and wonder seen in the eyes of young people who are passing through. The disparate sizes and hues of the aquatic life on display are genuinely uplifting.

The two *Sea Cliffs* areas outside of the indoor halls feature walruses and penguins, who are both in their own way engaging. A temporary home for turtles, rays and sand tiger sharks stands at the back of the *New York Aquarium* grounds, giving the visitor a glimpse of what will be when a much larger shark enclave is completed. The future *Ocean Wonders: Sharks* area is one of four attractions now under construction, all within areas closer to the shore, where Hurricane Sandy hit in 2012 and damaged the *Aquarium*. Beyond all this is the main highlight of the *New York Aquarium*, the fabulous *Aquatheater*.

Three times a day, the resident sea lions join with their trainers to present an extremely entertaining show. Set inside the circular *Aquatheater*, which holds around 200 people, the sea lion show offers a great chance to both take a break and enjoy the intelligence of these wonderful sea creatures. A small 4D Theater just outside the *Aquarium* entrance is another spot where visitors can sit down and enjoy a different type of sea life, in the form of a movie with refreshing outside effects.

The F and Q trains to West 8th Street leave you right across the street from *The New York Aquarium*. The D and N trains to Stillwell Avenue leave you a few blocks away. The B36 bus stops right in front of the *Aquarium,* on West 8th Street and Surf Avenue.

Walking Distance: Nathan' Famous; Cyclone Rollercoaster; Wonder Wheel; Luna Park; MCU Park; Coney Island Boardwalk.

The Meatball Shop

http://www.themeatballshop.com

In less than a decade, a wonderful chain of specialized foods has been growing in *The City*. *The Meatball Shop*, which originally opened in the Lower East Side in 2010, had added six (6) more locations by early 2017, each of which carried on with the promise that the franchise title suggests, that of really good meatballs… and a few other things.

Childhood friends Daniel Holzman and Michael Chernow took slightly different paths to teaming up with one another as co-owners of *The Meatball Shop*. Holzman had been in the cooking business since he was 15, and his time at the Culinary Institute of America led him to gigs at some notable restaurants like Palladin, Napa and The Campton Place. In 2010, he hooked up with his old buddy Chernow, to open *The Meatball Shop*. Chernow, who had been in the restaurant business since he was a teenager in the Upper East Side, enrolled in the French Culinary Institute in 2007. He graduated with honors and an associate's degree in both Culinary Arts and Restaurant Management, before he and Holzman got together The fact that two old friends are at the heart of this chain seems apropos, because *The Meatball Shop* does have a very friendly feel to it.

The brilliance of *The Meatball Shop* may be in the specific checklist menus that are offered. There are a handful of meatballs and sauces and a short list of side orders which can also be ordered "*under the balls*," so to speak. The brunch menu incorporates eggs and biscuits; there are sandwich choices on the basic menu and cookie-shell ice cream sandwiches on the dessert menu, with choices between five different cookies and ice creams. Beverages range from root beer floats to various cocktails. There are daily specials, as well. *The Meatball Shop* is a charming place, whether you eat at the shop or order food to go.

The Meatball Shop was such an immediate hit when it debuted in the Lower East Side in 2010, that shops in Chelsea, the West Village, the Upper East and West Sides and Williamsburg, Brooklyn, were opened in relatively short order. In March of 2017, a seventh shop opened in Hells' Kitchen. It would be of no surprise at all if more locations were to follow.

To get to *The Meatball Shop* at 84 Stanton Street in the Lower East Side (the original), take the F train to Delancey Street or 2nd Avenue, which are both a few blocks away, as is the Essex Street stop of the J, M and Z trains. The M15 bus stops right by the shop. Check *The Meatball Shop* website for directions to the other locations.

Walking Distance: 84 Stanton Street (Lower East Side): New Museum; Lower East Side Tenement Museum; Basilica at Old St. Patrick's Cathedral. 170 Bedford Avenue (Williamsburg, Brooklyn): McCarren Park; Knitting Factory Brooklyn; Music Hall of Williamsburg. 64 Greenwich Avenue (West Village): Village Vanguard; Washington Square Park; IFC Center. 200 Ninth Avenue (Chelsea): Irish Repertory Theatre; Flatiron Building; The Cell Theatre. 1462 Second Avenue (Upper East Side): Met Breuer; Comic Strip Live. 447 Amsterdam Avenue (Upper West Side): American Museum of Natural History; New-York Historical Society. 789 Ninth Avenue (Hell's Kitchen):Amy's Bread; Broadway Theatre District; Carolines on Broadway.

The Town Hall & the 92nd Street Y

https://thetownhall.org
https://www.92y.org

New York City is a place where one can go to a great show on Broadway, catch a professional ballgame in four different boroughs or find various musical or comedic talents in a number of different places. And if you would simply like to not only attend a performance, but a conversation with noted New Yorkers, educators or performers, there are two very busy sites that lead the way. Whether you choose *The Town Hall* of the *92nd Street Y*, you can be fairly certain that a thought-provoking and/or entertaining time will be experienced, whenever you enter either of these electric venues.

The Town Hall, located at 123 West 43rd Street, between 6th Avenue and Broadway, opened in 1921, as a space where people of all types could be educated on the issues of the day. *The Town Hall* also featured no box or obstructed view seats, spurring the motto: "*Not a bad seat in the house*." In its early days, women's suffrage and birth control were amongst its most controversial topics. From 1935-56, the radio program "*America's Town Meeting of the Air*" was produced by *The Town Hall*, with four speakers considering a pre-determined topic. Making its debut on Memorial Day, 1935, the *Town Meeting* became increasingly popular and eventually went on tour, both in the United States and on three continents. Poetry has also been a staple from the very beginning, with Edna St. Vincent Millay making her debut reading there in 1928. The acoustics in *The Town Hall* were thought by some performers to be superior to Carnegie Hall and as such, many Classical and Jazz acts have graced its corridors.

The *92nd Street Y*, located on 92nd Street and Lexington Avenue, is an even older multi-functional performance venue. Founded in 1874 as *The Young Men's Hebrew Association* by a group of Jewish-German professionals and business men, the *92nd Street Y* remains an organization which reflects Jewish principles, while serving people of all races and faiths. The Kauffman Concert Hall and the Buttenweiser Hall, both located within the 92nd Street venue, offer up a variety of talks, literary readings and concert performers. The *92nd Street Y's* School of the Arts features art, music, dance and creative writing for students of all ages, with various programs for children and adults which accentuate Jewish life, health & fitness and the arts.

The 1, 2, 3, N, Q, R and S trains to 42nd Street/Times Square all leave you a few blocks from *The Town Hall.* The 6 train to either 86th street or 96th Street leaves you a few blocks from the *92nd Street Y,* as do the M1, M2, M3, M4, M101, M102 and the M103 buses.

Walking Distance: **The Town Hall**: B.B. King's; Madame Tussaud's Wax Museum; Ripley's Believe It or Not Odditorium; Port Authority Bus Terminal; Broadway Theater District; Bryant Park; New York Public Library, Main Branch; Grand Central Terminal; Amy's Bread; Radio City Music Hall; Rockefeller Center; St. Patrick's Cathedral; Gulliver's Gate. **92nd Street Y**: Marx Brothers Place; Cooper Hewitt; National Academy; Solomon R. Guggenheim Museum; Jewish Museum; Central Park East.

Tompkins Square Park

https://www.nycgovparks.org/parks/tompkins-square-park/history

Many of the smaller parks in *The City* have long been places for gatherings and/or contemplation. One of these is *Tompkins Square Park* in the East Village, which contains a few diverse tributes and a quiet feel for history. *Tompkins* is in fact a square park, bordered by 7th Street, Avenue A, 10th Street and Avenue D. It sits right in the heart of an area that is still a haven for artists and activists.

Named after Daniel D. Tompkins (1774–1825), who served as Governor of New York from 1807 to 1817 and then as Vice President of the United States under the 5th U.S. President, James Monroe, the property was owned by the director general of the Dutch colony of New Netherland, Peter Stuyvesant, during the 17th century. Tompkins later acquired the land, which by the 19th century was targeted for development as a public square. A proposed market in 1811 never came to pass and in 1834, *The City* acquired the land. Originally swampland, this site was landscaped between 1835 and 1850. In 1866, a number of trees that had been planted at the time of the park's creation to allow for an open parade ground for the Seventh Regiment of New York were removed, though a few Sycamore trees were spared. Believed to be the oldest trees in the park, two of the Sycamores can be found along 10th Street and on Avenue A at 9th Street.

Tompkins Square Park is the home of a few memorials. The *Temperance Memorial Fountain* (1891) was a gift from a San Francisco dentist and temperance activist, Henry Cogswell (1820-1900). The *Samuel S. "Sunset" Fox* statue, dedicated to a man who was instrumental in securing paid benefits and a 40-hour work week to postal workers, was moved to the park in 1824, from its original site in nearby Astor Place (1891). The *Slocum Memorial Fountain* (1906) remembers the many children killed in the 1904 East River fire on the cruise ship General Slocum (the second largest disaster in New York City history, after 9/11). The *Ukrainian-American Flagstaff* was donated in 1842. And the *Hare Krishna Tree*, an American elm near the center of the park, recalls when spiritualists held the first recorded outdoor Hare Krishna chanting sessions outside of India in 1966. Also containing a dog walk and a children's play area, *Tompkins Square Park* is a small park that is rich with history.

The 6 train to Astor Place leaves you a short walk from *Tompkins Square Park.* The R or the W to 8th Street/Broadway stop a few blocks further away, but are well within walking distance. The M8 and M14A both stop near the park.

Walking Distance: Museum of the American Gangster; S'Mac; New Museum; Basilica at Old St. Patrick's Cathedral; The Meatball Shop.

United Nations

http://visit.un.org/content/tickets

Of the places in New York City that offer guided tours, one of the most interesting and well-constructed is the tour of the *United Nations*. Located on First Avenue, between 42nd and 46th Streets, the *United Nations* currently consists of 193 member states. The tour of the *United Nations* educates visitors and shows a fascinating panorama of ideas, art and perspectives of many nations around the world.

Founded in 1945, as World War II was coming to an end, the United Nations is an international organization that has in its charter maintaining international peace and security, protecting human rights, delivering humanitarian aid and upholding international law. The complex in Manhattan that serves as the *United Nations Headquarters*, a fascinating and iconic site on the shores of the East River, is a fabulous place to visit. From the history of the venue itself to the many facets of the *United Nations'* existence, the one-hour guided tour leaves one with a greater understanding of a place that should probably be more appreciated and supported.

The corridors of the *United Nations* are filled with permanent and traveling exhibits, which all seem to speak for the human condition. Once inside, you have full access to the halls before and after your tour. On the tour itself, a very professional guide takes you through the four main conference chambers, the Security Council, the Trusteeship Council Chamber, the Economic and Social Council and the one that the public is most familiar with, the General Assembly. Each is described as to mission and member states participating. Between visiting each council hall, there are many gifts from member states on display throughout the building, including sculptures, tapestries and other artistic presentations. In many ways, going to the *United Nations* is like visiting an art museum. The pieces are that exquisite and well presented. Notable ones include a display of framed Human Rights prints that take up an entire wall, a statue of St. Agnes recovered from the Nagasaki bomb site and a mosaic based on a Norman Rockwell painting.

Overall, taking the *United Nations* tour is a solid addition to any New Yorker's or City visitor's checklist of things to do. There is also a nice gift shop with an eclectic array of items to consider. It is important to note that you need a government-issued photo ID, such as a passport, to gain entry into the *United Nations*.

The 4, 5, 6 and 7 trains to Grand Central Terminal and the F and M trains to 42nd Street/Bryant Park leave you a few blocks from the *United Nations*, located on First Avenue, between 42nd and 46th Streets. The M15 and M42 buses stop a block away.

Walking Distance: Grand Central Terminal; Bryant Park; New York Public Library; The Town Hall.

Washington Square Park/Triangle Shirtwaist Factory site

www.washingtonsquareparkconservancy.org www.osha.gov/oas/trianglefactoryfire.html

One of the most endearing respites in *The City* is *Washington Square Park*, located in the heart of the New York University campus in Greenwich Village, bordered by Waverly Place, MacDougal Street, West 4th Street and University Place. This small patch of land has a charm that transcends most other relatively similar yards found in the five boroughs. The classic and familiar *Washington Square Arch* that serves as the de facto main entrance also marks the starting point of 5th Avenue and leads one into one of the most recognizable parks in New York.

The land west of what was once a marshy area known as Minetta Creek was turned into the Washington Military Parade Ground (public training spaces for volunteer militia defense companies) in 1826. By 1849-50, the parade ground was replaced by the first park to appear on the site. The recently chartered New York City Department of Parks took over in 1871 and replaced the old straight paths with the now familiar curved paths within the park. In 1889, a temporary *Arch,* made of plaster and wood, was constructed to commemorate the 100th anniversary of George Washington's inauguration as the first U.S. President. The permanent marble *Arch* that still stands today went up in 1892. Renovations in the 1930's and in recent times would shape the park. Today, *Washington Square Park's* most prominent features are a fountain in the center of the grounds, two dog walks and tables at the Northeast end of the park where chess players can be found matching wits on a daily basis. Also at the Northeast end of the park is the so-called "*Hangman's Tree*," an over 330-year old Elm which tangibly represents when hangings were purported to be done in this square long ago. The park has long been a haven for artists and musicians, with the 1960's folk movement representing its most memorable period.

A block off the eastern entrance of *Washington Square Park*, on Washington Place and Greene Street, is the former site of the *Triangle Shirtwaist Factory*, which today is NYU's Biology and Chemistry Building. On March 25, 1911, 146 workers, all young women, died in a fire in which locked exits trapped the workers inside. The tragic *Triangle Fire* resulted in unprecedented safety reforms for U.S. workers. The site was designated a National Historic Landmark in 1991 and there are three plaques commemorating the site, including one from the International Ladies Garment Workers Union. What was originally called the Asch Building is now known as the Brown Building, after Frederick Brown, who donated the building to New York University in 1929.

The R train to 8th Street leaves you just a few blocks from *Washington Square Park* and the *Triangle Shirtwaist Factory* site.

Walking Distance: Merchant's House Museum; Ukrainian Museum; The Meatball Shop; New Museum; Tompkins Square Park; S'Mac; The Basilica at Old St. Patrick's Cathedral; IFC Center; Film Forum.

Wonder Theatres

http://www.unitedpalace.org/upca http://www.kingstheatre.com

Many of us recall the days of grandiose, majestic movie houses in New York City, which began fading from sight in the 1970's and 80's. These days, the re-birth of some of these old palaces is a most welcome development. Back in 1929-30, in four of New York's boroughs and Jersey City, New Jersey, five so-called *Loew's Wonder Theatres* opened to great fanfare and approval. These houses offered full-length features on the big screen, along with live performances before and/or after the movies. They all stood tall for decades, before neglect and decay saw them all close down. But in recent times, a few have been reborn. Two of them, the *Paradise Theatre* in The Bronx and the *Valencia Theatre* in Queens, are currently utilized as churches. A third, the *Jersey Theatre* in Jersey City, has re-opened as a classic cinema theatre and performing arts center. And then there are the two *Wonder Theatres* located in Manhattan and Brooklyn.

The *United Palace*, known as the *Loew's 175th Street* when it opened in 1930 as the final *Wonder Theatre,* was purchased and preserved in 1969 by "prosperity preacher" Frederick J. Eikerenkoetter II, better known as Reverend Ike. Today, led by Reverend Ike's son, Xavier Eikerenkoetter, *United Palace* consists of three factions, the *United Palace House of Inspiration (UPHI),* the *United Palace of Cultural Arts (UPCA*), and the *United Palace Theatre (UPT).* Proceeds from the screening of classic movies and live performances help support the ministry.

The *Kings Theatre* at 1027 Flatbush Avenue in Brooklyn served as a first class movie theatre and live performance venue from 1930-1977, before it was closed down and abandoned for 36 years. In 2013, renovations began and in January of 2015, a Diana Ross concert re-opened the place in style. The *Kings Theatre* pulled off an almost miraculous re-birth, with decades of sometimes massive water damage throughout the theatre eliminated and the corridors and stairways restored to their former lavish style. The lobby has 7 original chandeliers and 11 pieces of original furniture from the Ladies Lounge were secured from an elderly woman who had acquired them when the theatre closed. Today, the *Kings Theatre* is used mostly for concerts and live performances, though they show a big screen movie on occasion. Both of these re-born *Wonder Theatres* are places that really need to be seen.

.

The A train to 175th Street leaves you two blocks from the *United Palace*. The Q train to Beverley Road is 6 blocks from the *Kings Theatre*, and the Church Street stops on the B, 2 and 5 trains are three blocks away. The B41 bus leaves you right by the *Kings Theatre.*

Walking Distance: 175th Street: J Hood Wright Park; Fort Washington Park; George Washington Bridge; Armory Track; Highbridge Park
Flatbush Avenue: Flatbush YMCA of Greater New York; Flatbush Library; Prospect Park

Inside Astoria Park in Queens, looking out over Astoria Pool, with the Hell Gate Bridge in the background.

The more than a century old Paymaster Building in the Brooklyn Navy Yard, where thousands of servicemen and women and civilian workers once got paid, is now the oldest active whiskey distillery in New York City.

The Basilica of St. Patrick's Old Cathedral at 263 Mulberry Street, now a neighborhood church, was built in the years 1809-1815 and served as the hub of the Catholic Church, before being superseded by the current St. Pat's in 1879.

The back porch of the Dyckman Farmhouse Museum on 204th Street, the oldest farmhouse in Manhattan.

The centerpiece of the Franklin D. Roosevelt Four Freedoms Park on Roosevelt Island is a huge bust of FDR.

The Hall of Fame for Great Americans on the Bronx Community College campus showcases 98 busts of prominent Americans.

St. Patrick's Cathedral on Fifth Avenue, between 50th and 51st streets, is the most celebrated church in The City.

The Flatiron Building on 175 Fifth Avenue, at East 22nd Street, is one of the most photographed sites in New York City.

The General Grant National Memorial, in Riverside Park on 122nd Street, is the largest mausoleum in North America.

The Hamilton Grange National Memorial at 141st Street in St. Nicholas Park, the final residence of Founding Father Alexander Hamilton.

The Hispanic Society of America Museum & Library on Broadway, between 155th and 156th Streets, on the campus of Boricua College.

Jane's Carousel in Brooklyn, with the Brooklyn Bridge in the background.

These plaques in Downtown Brooklyn celebrate the history of Brooklyn baseball. The 1860 Brooklyn Excelsiors called the house at 133 Clinton Street (above) home and Jackie Robinson signed his historic contract with the Brooklyn Dodgers in the team's old offices, which were once located at the corner of Montague and Court Streets, where the plaque below now resides.

The King Manor Museum in Jamaica, Queens, former home of Founding Father Rufus King, one of the signers of the Constitution.

The Lefferts Historic House Museum, inside Prospect Park, Brooklyn, offers up an example of life in Brooklyn in the early 1800's.

The Louis Armstrong House Museum at 34-56 107th Street in Corona, Queens, was the home of the legendary jazz musician from 1943 until his death in 1971.

At the top of the John T. Brush Stairway in Upper Manhattan, which was dedicated to the New York Giants owner in 1913, a year following his death. Refurbished in 2014, the Brush Stairway connects the top and bottom of Coogan's Bluff, making it easier for residents to navigate the surrounding Highbridge Park.

The Zoo Center at the Bronx Zoo is the centerpiece of The City's largest and most famous zoo.

Federal Hall at 26 Wall Street in Downtown Manhattan, where the statue of George Washington out front reminds visitors that this was where the First President of the United States took the oath of office on April 30, 1798.

The Edgar Allan Poe Cottage on the Grand Concourse and Kingsbridge Road in The Bronx was the final home of the tortured master poet and story teller.

The Imagine mosaic at Strawberry Fields in Central Park West, the tribute to slain Beatle John Lennon, just off 72nd Street.

The Mount Vernon Hotel Museum, located in the heart of The City, at 421 East 61st Street, was a lavish "country" resort hotel in the 1800's.

The Van Cortlandt House Museum in the park of the same name in The Bronx, once the home of one of the most affluent families in New York City.

Marx Brothers Place. The top floor of this building at 179 East 93rd Street was where the famous comedians lived from around 1895 to 1909.

(2)

Museums & Historic Houses

African Burial Ground National Monument

https://www.nps.gov/afbg/index.htm

In 1991, during the early stages of constructing a federal office building at 290 Broadway, African burial remains were found. Over the next two years, about an acre of what was a 6.6 acre cemetery was excavated, with 419 skeletal remains removed. A great controversy ensued as to how to honor the site, which a 1755 map called a "*Negro Burial Ground*." After numerous protest and town hall style meetings, an agreement was reached. Today, the result is the *African Burial Ground National Monument*, which has both indoor and outdoor components.

The outdoor memorial, which is closed from November 1 through March 31 each Winter, contains two sculptures, the *Circle of the Diaspora*, which charts the places where Africans came to this country from and the *Ancestral Chamber*, a contemplative area. Seven mounds where bones were re-interred, called the *Ancestral Re-interment Ground*, located behind the *Ancestral Chamber*, completes the sacred ground This most reflective area allows visitors to stand right over the grounds where African slaves were once buried.

In 2010, the indoor Visitors Center opened, with a 40-seat theatre, four exhibit areas and a bookstore. The centerpiece of the exhibits is a wonderful re-enactment of an African Funeral ceremony, as it might have looked in the 17th or 18th Centuries. Statues of three elders and a child surround a very small casket, which is clearly for a very young person. Other exhibits pan out all around this funeral scene, including two timelines, one of slavery as it existed in the New Amsterdam (York) area and another that charts the *African Burial Ground* area from discovery in 1991, through the trials that brought it to the present day. There is a research library to the rear of the building, which is available by appointment. In both the indoor Visitors Center and outdoor Memorial area, this most powerful historical American discovery can be explored by visitors on a daily basis.

The *African Burial Ground National Monument* is the first National Monument dedicated to Africans of early New York and Americans of African descent. The *African Burial Ground* itself had been designated a National Historic Landmark in 1993. In February of 2006, a full 100 years after the Antiquities Act of 1906 authorized the President to protect landmarks, structures, and objects of historic or scientific interest by designating them as National Monuments, 290 Broadway was named the *African Burial Ground National Monument.*

The 1, 2, 3, A and C trains to Chambers Street, the R and W trains to City Hall and the 4, 5 and 6 to Brooklyn Bridge/City Hall all leave you a few blocks from the *African Burial Ground National Monument.*

Walking Distance: Canyon of Heroes, Anne Frank Center New York; Brooklyn Bridge; One World Observatory; Federal Hall. Irish Hunger Memorial.

Alice Austen House (Clear Comfort)

http://aliceausten.org

In the entrance to New York Harbor, on the eastern shores of Staten Island, there stands a home built in the late 1600's which today celebrates its most famous resident. From the front porch of the *Alice Austen House*, there is a wonderful view of the Verrazano-Narrows Bridge to the right and a tangible notion of how it once felt to live in this seaside home, known in its time as *Clear Comfort*.

Alice Austen was one of the first prominent female photographers. Born in 1866, she and her mother moved in with her maternal grandparents when Alice was very young, after her father abandoned them. Her grandfather, John Haggerty Austen, had purchased the home in 1844 and his wife Elizabeth quickly dubbed it "*Clear Comfort*." John Austen, who originally imagined the place (built in 1690 as a one-room Dutch cottage) as a Summer home, brought his entire family to live there permanently in 1852. He would continue to renovate and add rooms, including a second floor, over a 25-year period. More importantly for young Alice, one of those who called *Clear Comfort* home was Oswald Muller, who was married to her mother's younger sister Mary (known as "Aunt Minn"). A clipper ship captain, Uncle Oswald introduced Alice to photography when she was 10-years old. By the time she was 18, she was an expert photographer.

Alice Austen produced over 8,000 images, many of her home and Staten Island itself, though she did take an extensive collection of pictures of immigrants in Manhattan, often hauling up to 50 pounds of equipment to take her photos. *Clear Comfort* would remain in the Austen family for just over 100 years, before Alice and her longtime partner, Gertrude Tate, who'd lived with her since 1917, were forced to sell in 1945. The building fell into disarray, but in the 1960's a local group helped save the home and renovate it, for use as a museum.

Re-named the *Alice Austen House*, the historic home was included in the National Register of Historic Places in 1970, was designated a New York City Landmark in 1971 and became a National Historic Landmark in 1993. Today, it showcases two period rooms and Alice's second floor darkroom and is the site of a number of educational programs.

The 1 train to South Ferry, the 4 and 5 to Bowling Green and the R and W to Whitehall Street/South Ferry all leave you by the Manhattan entrance to the Staten Island Ferry. From the St. George Terminal in Staten Island, you take the S51 bus to Bay Street and Hylan Boulevard, which leaves you two blocks from the water and the Alice Austen House at 2 Hylan Boulevard.

Walking Distance: Garibaldi Meucci Museum.

Brooklyn Navy Yard (BLDG 92)

http://bldg92.org

Of all the legendary sites in New York City, one had fallen out of the conversation in the past few decades. But in recent times, with new businesses and a brand new visitors' center and museum, the *Brooklyn Navy Yard* is once again something to talk about.

Also known as the *United States Navy Yard* and the *New York Naval Shipyard (NYNS),* the *Brooklyn Navy Yard* opened in 1806 and served as a shipbuilding and ship repair outlet until 1966, when it was closed down, along with many other military installations which were deemed non-essential. In its time, the *Brooklyn Navy Yard* produced some of the most famous naval vessels in U.S. history, including the USS Arizona, built during World War I and fated to become the symbol of the Pearl Harbor attack of December 7, 1941 and the USS Missouri, the ship on which the Japanese would surrender to the Allied powers, ending WWII. But it was the notable efforts of the *Brooklyn Navy Yard's* 70,000 workers, in the field of ship repairing during World War II that earned the yard the nickname "*The Can-Do Shipyard.*"

The legacy of the *Brooklyn Navy Yard* is even more widespread. The Brooklyn Naval Hospital, adjacent to the yard, operated from the Civil War through World War II and was one of the oldest naval hospitals in the United States when it closed in the mid-1970's. Seatrain Shipbuilding operated within the yard from 1967-79. For years after that, some businesses, notably a film studio, utilized areas within the yard.

In 2011, the *Brooklyn Navy Yard Center at BLDG 92* opened as a visitors' center and museum dedicated to the past, present and future of the *Brooklyn Navy Yard.* The massive anchor of the Brooklyn born amphibious transport dock ship USS Austin greets you as you enter *BLDG 92* and a plaque honoring those who died in the 1960 fire of the USS Constellation within the yard's confines is located right outside. Themed bus tours of the yard are now run from *BLDG 92* and many new businesses are opening, among them the oldest whiskey distillery in New York City (circa 2010), which operates out of the over a century old Paymaster Building, where service men and women and civilian workers once picked up their wages. A visit to *BLDG 92* or taking a tour of the old *Brooklyn Navy Yard* is a most welcome addition to New York tourism, one which does *The City* proud.

The B57 and B69 buses stop near *BLDG 92* at 63 Flushing Avenue. The A or E to High Street or the F train to York Street leave you about a 10 minute walk to *BLDG 92.*

Walking Distance: Commodore Barry Park; Fort Greene Park; Manhattan Bridge; Brooklyn Bridge.

Cooper Hewitt

http://www.cooperhewitt.org

One of the more progressive museums located along the famous "*Museum Mile*" on 5th Avenue and Central Park is the *Cooper Hewitt Smithsonian Design Museum*, which is really a living, breathing tribute to creativity. Located on 91st Street since 1976, on the site of legendary steel baron Andrew Carnegie's 64-room Mansion, *Cooper Hewitt* allows visitors to not only view different designing styles and approaches, but also to take a shot at personally designing something themselves.

Cooper Hewitt is the only museum in the nation devoted exclusively to historic and contemporary design. The impact of design on daily life is addressed through various educational programs. Founded in 1897 by industrialist Peter Cooper's granddaughters Amy, Eleanor, and Sarah Hewitt, the museum has been a branch of the Smithsonian since 1967, one of only two Smithsonian branches located in New York City, along with the *George Gustav Heye Center*, which houses the *National Museum of the American Indian* in Bowling Green.

There are more than 200,000 design artifacts in the *Cooper Hewitt* collection, which also features a state of the art design library. Both historic and contemporary design is considered at *Cooper Hewitt* and the museum annually sponsors the National Design Awards, a highly regarded program which honors innovation and excellence in American design. Recent renovations began in 2008, with *Cooper Hewitt* re-opening on December 12, 2014. A terrace and garden, which was renovated in 2015, are also part of the *Cooper Hewitt* site.

Upon entering *Cooper Hewitt*, visitors are given a special pen which, when pressed up in a certain manner against the museum's exhibits, saves a photo of the particular exhibit that is then kept in an online file that is owned exclusively by the visitor. A sticker, also given upon entering, contains the unique webpage on the *Cooper Hewitt* site, which corresponds with all the data accumulated on the pre-programmed pen. This is a very innovative idea which I utilized to save 48 photos that I later accessed when I got home. The pen can also be used in a new part of the museum, *The Immersion Room*, where you can draw your own designs on a programmed table. *The Immersion Room* also allows a visitor to access *Cooper Hewitt's* vast collection of wallpapers, which project on the walls. *Cooper Hewitt* is a great place for the imagination to run free, something sorely needed in this age of push button results and instant gratification.

The 6 train to 86th Street and/or 96th Street leaves you just a few blocks from the *Cooper Hewitt Smithsonian Design Museum.* The M1, M2, M3 or M4 buses on Fifth and Madison Avenues and the crosstown M86 and M96 buses all have stops within walking distance.

Walking Distance: National Academy; Solomon R. Guggenheim Museum; Neue Galerie; Metropolitan Museum of Art; Central Park Great Lawn; Jewish Museum; Marx Brothers Place & Playground.

Discovery Times Square Museum

http://www.discoverytsx.com

Billing itself as "*More than a Museum*" might seem a bit haughty, but that description really does fit the *Discovery Times Square Museum (DTS)*, located at 226 West 44th Street, between 7th and 8th Avenues. The *DTS* is, in fact, part museum and part classroom, as various exhibitions that have graced its halls have proven, again and again. Located in an area that is as replete with human activity as anywhere in the world, this almost hidden in the side street venue offers up a variety of entertaining productions which reflect on the human condition, sometimes in a most extreme way.

Since opening in 2009, *Discovery Times Square* has featured such fascinating limited-time exhibits as *Titanic: the Artifact Exhibition, Leonardo Da Vinci's Workshop, King Tut: Return of the King, Pompeii: the Exhibit* and *Dead Sea Scrolls.* Those titles alone should conjure up plenty of imagery for the potential visitor. The payoff is that *DTS* delivers on that promising and anticipatory feeling that such historically-based amalgamations tend to render. For instance, the Titanic exhibit contained a large chunk of glacial ice that one could literally touch and in some abstract way feel the fate of the famous "unsinkable" ship, which was probably doomed from the moment it was given that moniker. There was also filmed footage of a salvage crew recovering 100-year old items from the Titanic (fine China, jewelry, clothing) which were now right there in the halls of *DTS,* for you to see, live and in person. Similarly, the Pompeii exhibit was riveting, as replicas of the bodies found encased in volcanic ash in the destroyed city of Pompeii, following the fateful eruption of Mount Vesuvius in 79 A.D., brought the visitor frightfully close to as infamous a human tragedy as has ever occurred.

What makes *Discovery Times Square* unique is that to complement these historically-based exhibitions, *DTS* offers up others which derive directly from modern pop culture. *Harry Potter: The Exhibition* and *CSI: The Experience,* two recent former residents of *DTS*, are good examples of this. More recent exhibits, *Body Worlds: Pulse* and *The Hunger Games: The Exhibition,* further illustrate the continuing diverse nature of *Discovery Times Square*. All of the displays and limited-run exhibits have interactive elements to them, which gives the visitor a unique educational experience. Television's *Discovery Channel* is the Official National Broadcast partner of *Discovery Times Square*, a most enjoyable and ever-evolving venue in *The City's* most accessible area.

The A, C and E trains to 42nd Street/Port Authority and the 1, 2, 3, N, Q, R and S trains to 42nd Street/Times Square all leave you a few blocks from the *Discovery Times Square Museum.*

Walking Distance: Broadway Theater District; Hard Rock Café; B.B. King's; Madame Tussaud's Wax Museum; Ripley's Believe it or Not Odditorium; New Victory Theatre; New York Public Library; Carolines on Broadway; The Town Hall; Bryant Park; Grand Central Terminal; Port Authority Bus Terminal; Intrepid Sea, Air & Space Museum; Circle Line; Gulliver's Gate.

Downtown Brooklyn Baseball Landmarks

http://www.thenationalpastimemuseum.com/article/brooklyn-excelsiors-baseballs-first-road-gang
http://www.theclio.com/web/entry?id=19299

Although it disappeared from the landscape for over 40 years, from 1958 to 2001, professional baseball in Brooklyn has always maintained a very large presence in the National Pastime. The Brooklyn Dodgers (1890-1957) left behind a fabled legacy that has sustained not only those old enough to have seen them play at Ebbets Field, but also to the sons and daughters of the Flatbush Faithful who have since been enchanted by the stories of their elders. The arrival of the Short Season Single "A" Brooklyn Cyclones off the shores of Coney Island in 2001 not only brought pro ball (though of the Minor League variety) back to the place where Jackie Robinson once helped change society, it also gave whole new generations of fans a chance to experience the magic of Brooklyn baseball, which dates back to even before the Dodgers first took the field in 1890. And in downtown Brooklyn, there are a couple of plaques, located just a few blocks from one another, which commemorate the rich legacy of the Borough of Churches.

In the early days of baseball, New York and Brooklyn, then a separate city, each had a significant presence. In Brooklyn, there were a number of semi-pro and pro outfits, with the most noteworthy being the Brooklyn Atlantics and the Brooklyn Excelsiors. The Excelsiors, in particular, left an indelible mark. In a time of mostly local games amongst baseball "club" teams, the Excelsiors were the first team to go on the road, in 1860, first to upstate New York in July and then to Philadelphia and Baltimore, in September. Whenever they returned home to Brooklyn, they stayed at a boarding house at 133 Clinton Street, which remains there today, with a plaque commemorating its most famous residents, including Jim Creighton, the earliest of Brooklyn's pitching greats.

About four blocks from the lesser known 133 Clinton Street is the former site of 215 Montague Street, which was where the Brooklyn Dodgers had their business offices from 1938-57. That building is gone now, but a bank on the same corner, at 212 Montague, also features a commemorative plaque which speaks to the glory days of Brooklyn baseball. The plaque celebrates the first meeting between Branch Rickey and Jackie Robinson, which would ultimately result in the integration of Major League baseball. For many believers in the soul of Brooklyn baseball, these plaques of Downtown Brooklyn represent not only former glory, but the hopes of greatness that may yet arrive.

The Borough Hall Station, where the 2, 3, 4, 5, N and R trains run, leaves you right across the street from the Jackie Robinson plaque and just a few blocks to 133 Clinton Street.

Walking Distance: Brooklyn Historical Society Museum; New York Transit Museum; Brooklyn Promenade; Metrotech Business Improvement District; Fulton Mall; Brooklyn War Memorial; Cobble Hill Cinemas.

Dyckman Farmhouse Museum

http://dyckmanfarmhouse.org

If you go way uptown to Inwood, you also can span the ages, to when most of Manhattan was countryside. The *Dyckman Farmhouse Museum* is the oldest farmhouse in Manhattan. Located just above a bus stop which delivers city travelers to and from more concrete venues, the *Dyckman Farmhouse Museum* transports you to the rural roots of this Upper Manhattan area, through a rather well preserved structure.

William Dyckman, the grandson of Patriarch Jan Dyckman (who had arrived in New Amsterdam in the 1600's from Westphalia) built the farmhouse in 1785 on his inherited family land, now on 204th Street and Broadway. When William died in 1787, his son Jacobus took over the house and farm, after the family initially advertised the property for sale. The house, which stayed in the family for several generations, until it was sold in 1868, was bought back by the family in 1915. After some restorations were done, they transferred ownership of the house to the City of New York in 1916, which opened it as a museum of Dutch and Colonial life, featuring the original Dyckman family furnishings.

There is a very small, winding staircase that leads to the basement, which served as a "winter" kitchen, removed from the elements above, as it were. Many cooking and preparation implements fill that area today. Another tight stairway takes you to the second floor, where a couple of bedrooms and a very narrow study are the attractions. Like in many centuries old homes in New York, the ceilings are very low in many places, which at *Dyckman* made guests speculate through the years that people surely must have been much shorter once. A parlor on the main floor features a classic desk, one like Jacobus Dyckman might have once used.

The *Dyckman Farmhouse Museum* has a great back porch that once led to the farm itself, though now there's just a garden out back. A view of the porch gives one the greatest feel for the times the house represents. In July of 1967, the *Dyckman Farmhouse Museum* was made a New York City Landmark and on Christmas Eve of that year, it was designated a National Historic Landmark and placed on the National Register of Historic Places. In 2016, the museum held a year-long 100th Anniversary celebration. It is one of 23 sites on the Historic House Trust of New York City and like all its sister houses, it is a great place to take groups of young people

The final stop on the A train, 207th Street, leaves you a block away from the *Dyckman Farmhouse Museum.* The 1 rain to 207th Street is just a few blocks away. The M100 and Bx7 buses stop right on 204th Street.

Walking Distance: The Met Cloisters at Fort Tryon Park; The Church of the Good Shepherd; Hudson River; Harlem River; Inwood Hill Park.

Federal Hall

https://www.nps.gov/feha/index.htm

One of the most famous spots in American History is located at the heart of the financial district in Lower Manhattan. *Federal Hall*, at 26 Wall Street, is a familiar spot to tourists, due to the statue of George Washington which stands tall on the steps of the building. Unfortunately, many people passing by simply take pictures of the statue and/or the *Federal Hall* building itself, without actually going inside to explore what is a very informative small museum.

The original *Federal Hall* building was constructed in 1699 as the second City Hall in New York City. Among the significant events there occurred here was in 1735, when John Peter Zenger, an American newspaper publisher, was imprisoned and tried there for committing libel against the British Royal Governor. Zenger was acquitted on the grounds that the material he had printed was considered freedom of the press as it was later defined in the Bill of Rights. After the American Revolution, this City Hall served as the meeting place for the Congress of the Confederation of the United States under the Articles of Confederation, from 1785 until 1789. In 1788, the building was remodeled and enlarged under the direction of Pierre Charles L'Enfant, who later designed the street grid in Washington, D.C. The building was renamed *Federal Hall* when it became the first Capitol of the United States under the Constitution in 1789. The 1st United States Congress met there on March 4, 1789 to establish the new federal government, and their first act was to tally the votes that elected George Washington as the first President of the United States.

On April 30, 1798, the Inauguration of Washington as the first United States President became the signature event ever held at *Federal Hall*. The original building was demolished in 1812. It was replaced in 1842 by the current structure, which served as the US

Customs House from 1842 to 1862. In 1882, the now iconic bronze statue of George Washington was erected on its front steps, on the approximate site where Washington was inaugurated as President. On May 26, 1939, the building was given the designation *Federal Hall Memorial National Historic Site*. On August 11, 1955, it was designated a National Memorial and on December 21, 1965, it was also designated a landmark by the New York City Landmarks Preservation Commission. Finally, on October 15, 1966, *Federal Hall* was added to the National Register of Historic Places. The current site is now officially known as the *Federal Hall National Monument*.

The 2, 3, 4 and 5 trains to Wall Street leave you a block from *Federal Hall*. The 1 and R trains to Rector Street leave you one block further away.

Walking Distance: Museum of American Finance; South Street Seaport District; Pier 6 Helicopter Tours; 9/11 Memorial & Museum; One World Observatory; Skyscraper Museum; Museum of Jewish Heritage; National Museum of the American Indian; Battery Park; Canyon of Heroes; Fraunces Tavern & Museum; Statue of Liberty/ Ellis Island Ferries; Staten Island Ferry.

Fraunces Tavern & Museum

http://www.fraunces tavern.com

Maybe the best hybrid historical venue in New York City, *Fraunces Tavern & Museum* at 54 Pearl Street on the southern tip of Manhattan is a place where you can tour a museum that looks back on the American Revolution, then sit down for a great meal. A very special site in the history of New York and the United States, *Fraunces Tavern* really does have a unique aura to it.

The first building erected on the current site went up in 1719. Until 1762, it was used as a dance studio and hall, for mercantile purposes and as a residential address. Samuel Fraunces purchased the land in 1762 and opened the first watering hole on the site, the *Sign of Queen Charlotte (Queen's Head Tavern)*, named for England's Queen Charlotte. In 1765, Fraunces leased management of the *Tavern*, but reclaimed it in 1770. In 1775, as the rebellion against England started to heat up, Fraunces moved to Elizabeth, New Jersey, leaving the operation of the *Tavern* to his Loyalist son-in-law, Charles Campbell, during the British occupation. Of course, the war turned and by 1783, Fraunces returned. On December 4, 1783, nine days after the final British troops left New York City, George Washington held a now famous farewell dinner for the officers of the Continental Army in the second floor Long Room. Through the late 1700's, the Department of War and the department of Foreign Affairs occupied space within the *Tavern.* Throughout the 1800's, it was a boarding house for the most part. The City claimed eminent domain in 1903, designating it a park to save the building, before selling it to the Sons of the Revolution in the State of New York (SRNY) in 1904.

The *Fraunces Tavern & Museum* opened in 1907, with four surrounding buildings added to the museum complex in the 1940's through the 1960's. In 1965, the site was designated a New York City Landmark and in 2008, 54 Pearl Street was added to the National

Register of Historic Places. Today, the museum on the second and third floors showcases artifacts from the American Revolution, along with the history of the Sons of the Revolution. The restaurant and bar occupy a few rooms on the main floor, with a very popular Happy Hour each day, as well as various live performances on weekends, from Jazz to Rock and Roll to Traditional Irish Folk music. Steeped in history, with an upbeat atmosphere, the *Fraunces Tavern & Museum* is a splendid place to spend an afternoon.

The 1 train to South Ferry and the R and W trains to Whitehall Street leave you just a few blocks from the *Fraunces Tavern & Museum.*

Walking Distance: Museum of American Finance; Federal Hall; South Street Seaport District; Pier 6 Helicopter Tours; 9/11 Memorial & Museum; One World Observatory; Skyscraper Museum; Museum of Jewish Heritage; National Museum of the American Indian; Battery Park; Canyon of Heroes; Statue of Liberty/Ellis Island Ferries; Staten Island Ferry.

General Grant National Memorial

https://www.nps.gov/gegr/index.htm

The largest mausoleum in North America celebrates one of the most revered figures in American history. The *General Grant National Memorial*, located in Riverside Park on 122nd Street provides a solemn, yet inspiring look at Ulysses S. Grant, the man universally credited with saving the Union during the Civil War, before becoming the 18th President of the United States.

A West Point graduate who served unceremoniously in the Mexican-American War, he retired in 1854. He re-enlisted in 1861 and his seemingly unlikely ascendancy into American folklore began when President Abraham Lincoln named him the head of the Union forces in 1864, succeeding a number of other generals who were not up to the task. Grant's tactical genius and unflappable cool under pressure is what separated him from his predecessors. Defeating the revered Robert E. Lee and thus keeping the Union intact, Grant further distinguished himself by his extremely compassionate treatment of the fallen Confederate Army, during the historic Grant-Lee surrender summit at Appomattox Courthouse. A small mural of Grant and Lee is on display inside the *General Grant National Monument*, or *Grant's Tomb*, which the majestic mausoleum is more frequently called.

Grant spent two terms as President (1869-77), highlighted by his signing of the act that made Yellowstone Park the country's first National Park. When he died in 1885, his funeral procession in New York City took five hours and was attended in the streets by over a million people. The idea of a special resting place came to fruition on July 27, 1897, which would have been Grant's 75th birthday. That day, the dedication ceremony for the *General Grant National Memorial* was led by President McKinley and attended by dignitaries from 26 countries. When his wife Julia died in 1902, her matching casket was situated right next to Grant's.

In addition to the Grants' remains, the mausoleum contains flags from assorted Union regiments and busts of a number of other Civil War generals, including one of General William Tecumseh Sherman, Grant's great friend, who is situated to be looking directly at the Grants' caskets. There is a visitors' center across the street and some fabulous mosaic tile benches around one side of the memorial. Grant's simple inauguration day message, "*Let us have peace*," adorns the facing of the edifice. A more fitting tribute to an American hero you will not find.

To get to the *General Grant National Memorial*, take the 1 train to 116th Street, walk up Broadway to 122nd Street, turn left and walk two blocks. The M11 bus to Amsterdam Avenue and West 118th Street and the M104, M4 or M5 buses to 122nd Street and Broadway all leave you a few blocks away.

Walking Distance: Riverside Park; The Riverside Church; Columbia University; Morningside Park; Nicholas Roerich Museum.

Hamilton Grange National Memorial

https://www.nps.gov/hagr/index.htm

At the turn of the 19th Century, the majority of Manhattan's population lived downtown, in what is today the Financial District. The spread of Yellow Fever in the crowded Summer streets and the desire to live in a more rural area sent many prominent citizens to the countryside in the northern reaches of the island. And so it was that Founding Father Alexander Hamilton built the only home he would ever own, within a 32-acre plot of land he purchased. As fate would have it, Hamilton only lived in this house for a few years. But *Hamilton Grange* has survived two centuries and a pair of moves to become a most vivid memorial of the times of America's first Secretary of the Treasury.

Built in 1802, *Hamilton Grange*, named after Alexander's father's ancestral home in Scotland, was constructed in the favored Federalist-style architecture of the day. Hamilton and his wife, Elizabeth, had decided to buy some land and move into the Harlem Heights neighborhood after a number of enjoyable visits with friends who lived in the area. The 90-minute carriage ride that brought him to and from his workplace Downtown was well worth it for Hamilton, who liked the cool breezes that were a welcome feature of his new neighborhood. The many parties in their new home ended abruptly when Hamilton was killed in his infamous duel with Aaron Burr in 1804. Elizabeth lived there until 1835, when she moved to Washington, D.C., where she died at age 97 in 1854.

The current location of the *Hamilton Grange National Memorial* at 141st Street in St. Nicholas Park is the result of two moves. In 1899, when the City grid finally reached that far Uptown, with the *Grange* right in the path of the construction, St. Luke's Church saved the building by moving it two blocks south, right next to the church. This site became a museum in 1924. In 2008, the *Grange* was moved around the corner and down one steep block into St. Nicholas Park, where porches, which were eliminated to accommodate the limited area of the second site, were restored. They show a great video of the 2008 move as part of the 45-minute guided tour that the Parks Service offers at *Hamilton Grange*.

To get to the *Hamilton Grange National Memorial*, take the 1 train to 137th Street, walk up Broadway to 141st Street, turn right and walk three blocks. The A, B, C and D trains to 145th Street also leave you a few blocks away. The M3 bus stops at 141st Street and St. Nicholas Avenue and the M4, M5 (Broadway), M100 and M101 (Amsterdam) buses have stops on 141st Street, a few blocks away.

Walking Distance: St. Luke's Episcopal Church; City College of New York (CCNY); Riverbank State Park; Jackie Robinson Park.

Hispanic Society Museum and Library

http://hispanicsociety.org

If you take a trip to the Upper West Side, to an area called the Audubon Terrace, there is a fabulous showcase within the environs of Boricua College. The *Hispanic Society of America Museum and Library*, located on Broadway, between 155th and 156th Streets, offers up some wonderful history from Spain and Latin America. It was founded in 1904 by Archer Milton Huntington, who sought to establish a free, public museum and library that would study, through art and sculpture, the culture of Spain, Latin America and the Philippines. More than a century later, with a statue of Castilian nobleman and military leader El Cid seemingly standing guard outside, one can see that Huntington achieved this goal with flying colors.

The Museum and Library collections cover nearly every aspect of art and culture in Spain, Portugal, Latin America, and the Philippines into the 20th century. This scope of the collection of Hispanic works is second only to that of ones in Spain itself. Detailed sculptures take up much of the main floor and epic paintings line the mezzanine balcony just above it. Masters like El Greco and Goya are represented, as are various other lesser known artists. Upon entering the main hall with the mezzanine above, the feeling of an ancient culture is palpable. The reddish-brown walls above play off the decorative arches that line the ground floor in a way that is both visceral and imaginative. Of all the smaller museums that I have been to, the *Hispanic Society Museum* has the greatest *feel* to it, one that inspires the thoughts of the times represented.

There is a featured gallery room to the right of the main hall and at the time of my visit, the walls of this gallery featured absolutely stunning murals by Joaquin Sorolla y Bastida (1863-1923), under the title "Vision of Spain." By viewing the 360 degree panorama images in the gallery, Sorolla tells the story of the Spanish people in graphic detail. Adjoining rooms from the mezzanine showcased porcelain plates and vases and housed more mundane things like storage trunks and furniture from as far back as the 17th Century. This most powerful museum is complimented by a research library which contains manuscripts, atlases, charts and rare books. The *Hispanic Society* holds a number of learning programs, concerts and lectures, right there inside the museum proper. It is a remarkable resource for anyone who wishes to learn of the cultures of Spain and Latin America.

The 1 train to 157th Street and the C train to 155th Street leave you right by the *Hispanic Society of America Museum and Library.* The M4 and M5 buses stop at 155th Street and Broadway, as well.

Walking Distance: Trinity Church Cemetery & Mausoleum; Church of the intercession; John T. Brush Stairway; Morris-Jumel Mansion; Wright Brothers Playground; Dance Theatre of Harlem.

Italian American Museum (IAM)

http://www.italianamericanmuseum.org

A wonderful establishment that speaks of the immigrant experience is the *Italian American Museum*, located at 155 Mulberry Street, in the heart of Little Italy. On the site of what was once the *Banca Stabila* (*Stabile Bank*), which also served the Italian immigrant community as a post office, travel agent and all-around go-to information center, the *IAM* celebrates those of Italian descent in a most prideful and reflective manner.

In the two aisles that make up the modest *Italian American Museum*, there are various artifacts which speak to a number of contributions that the Italian people who came to America brought with them. Music is represented in a display about legendary singer Enrico Caruso, as well as a weathered accordion and an ancient organ grinder's music box. Law enforcement is highlighted by the story of crusading New York Police Lieutenant Joseph Petrosino, who was murdered by the pre-Mafia Black Hand while on assignment in Palermo, Italy in 1909. The tale of 1970's whistleblowing cop Frank Serpico honors more recent times. Merchants, street cleaners and transit workers are also in the panorama that is the *Italian American Museum*. The century old clerk's windows of the *Banca Stabila* are still intact and the original safe, which held hundreds of envelopes that immigrants left their valuables in (a sort of early safe deposit box) points out how much this venue once meant to Italian immigrants, as it should again today.

The idea for this museum came about during a 1999 exhibit at the New York-Historical Society called "*The Italians of New York: Five Centuries of Struggle and Achievement*." In 2001, Dr. Joseph Scelsa, the founder and President of the museum received the charter for the *IAM*. Dr. Scelsa, a delightful gentleman, remains on site still to greet and discuss anything about the Italian experience or any other historical New York institutions. There is also an exhibition/ screening room in the *IAM*, where artists are showcased and movies are screened. They have educational programs and seminars and there is a 7-minute movie they play, featuring Dr. Scelsa, which tells the story of the museum and its exhibits. The feast of *San Gennaro*, which was a must for all New Yorkers through the 1980's, before becoming more of the street fair that it is today, is duly noted at *IAM*.

The Canal Street stations of the 4, 6, B, D, J, N, Q, R and Z trains all leave you just a short walk from the corner of Mulberry and Grand Streets, where the *Italian American Museum* is located. The M5 bus to Broadway and Grand Street and the M103 bus to Bowery and Grand Street also leave you right near the *IAM*.

Walking Distance: Canal Street; Museum of Chinese in America (MOCA); Lower East Side Tenement Museum; Leslie-Lohman Museum of Gay and Lesbian Art; Museum at Eldridge Street; The Drawing Center.

Jewish Museum

http://thejewishmuseum.org

Another of the fascinating museums on Manhattan's Museum Mile is the *Jewish Museum,* located on 92nd Street, at 1009 Fifth Avenue, which features a wealth of diverse objects pertaining to the Jewish people of the world. It is the leading Jewish museum in the United States, with over 30,000 artifacts in its collections. Of the many ethnically-based museums in *The City*, the *Jewish Museum* has a most polished feel to it, as to the layout of the exhibits and their connection to the Jewish people.

The museum sits on the former of site of the Felix M. Warburg House, which was built for the philanthropist in 1908 by architect C.P.H. Gilbert. Warburg died in 1937 and the house was eventually donated by his family, in 1944, to become the permanent home of the *Jewish Museum.* The museum opened to the public in May of 1947 and saw expansions of the site in both 1963 and 1993. Today, the museum remains a fixture in the vast domain of world-class New York City museums.

There are four floors of galleries in the *Jewish Museum.* The first two floors are utilized for temporary exhibits and the third and fourth floors are reserved for the permanent exhibits which effectively portray the Jewish experience, both worldwide and here in the United States. Throughout the museum, portraits permeate the scene, as the Curator and Helen Goldsmith Menschel Director of the *Jewish Museum*, Claudia Gould, noted in the Spring & Summer 2015 Guide, "*The Jewish Museum's renowned collection includes hundreds of portraits by artists from the 18th Century to today.*" Beyond the portraits, the permanent displays also offer a wide-ranging collection of impressive religious artifacts, from antique menorahs to handcrafted Torahs, which all blend in to help preserve Jewish history and culture.

Becoming a member of the *Jewish Museum* offers one a number of great programs to consider. Every year, the museum hosts the *New York Jewish Film Festival;* the 2016 version offered a 25th Anniversary Festival. The historical significance of the old Warburg Mansion can be tangibly shared by hosting an event at the museum, from a company party to a bar or bat mitzvah. There are also travel programs available to members, as well as a fine gift shop open to the public, adjacent to the main building. The *Jewish Museum* is another venue that I would highly recommend.

The 6 train to either 86th Street or 96th Street leaves you a few blocks from the *Jewish Museum.* The Fifth Avenue M1, M2, M3 or M4 downtown buses stop across the street from the venue and the same buses, heading uptown on Madison Avenue, leave you just a block or two away.

Walking Distance: Cooper Hewitt; National Academy; Solomon R. Guggenheim Museum; Neue Galerie; Metropolitan Museum of Art; Central Park Great Lawn; Marx Brothers Place & Playground.

King Manor Museum

http://historichousetrust.org/house/king-manor-museum

All of the historic houses standing in New York City seem to have a particular trait that defines the home. The *King Manor Museum*, located at 153rd Street and Jamaica Avenue in Queens, features huge rooms throughout, be it main parlors or guest rooms. Due to the fact that it was the home of an individual who had a very tangible impact on American history, maybe that is exactly as it should be.

Rufus King was a founding father, one of the signers of the Constitution, a respected Senator from New York and one of the early voices who railed against slavery. From 1796-1803, King was appointed Ambassador to Great Britain. Returning to America following that assignment, he and his wife, Mary, bought this house in 1805, along with 90 acres of surrounding farmland. He expanded his new home to 29 rooms and the farm to 150 acres. When Rufus died in 1927, his son, John, bought the house and farm from his father's estate. He lived there for over 40 years, during which time he was elected Governor of New York, serving from 1857-59. Continuing his father's legacy, Governor King fought to arrest all those who tried to kidnap free black New Yorkers and sell them into slavery. John's daughter, Cornelia, was the final family member to live in the King Manor; she died there in 1896. The Village of Jamaica then bought the house and the 11.5 acres of land around it that was still owned by the King family. In 1900, the *King Manor Museum* was opened to the public.

The *King Manor Museum* is at the center of *Rufus King Park*, which is on the land that was purchased after Cornelia King's death. Inside, they offer very meticulous guided tours. Since the finished house was the sum total of three separate structures that were all connected by 1810, the walk through the halls of the family side of the home to the servants' entrances and working areas is particularly long. The corridors and hallways are wide and vast and the rooms are all noticeably robust. Period furniture mixes with the original wooden floors and fireplaces in almost every room. As a bonus, one room contains a timeline history of the Village of Jamaica during the time that John King owned the house. There are concerts and educational events held in the ample presentation space that the *King Manor Museum* provides.

The E, J and Z trains to Jamaica Center leave you two blocks from the *King Manor Museum*, as do the following buses, which all stop on Archer Avenue, right outside the subway station: Q24, Q42, Q43, Q44, Q54, Q56, Q65 and the Q83.

Walking Distance: Jamaica Center Business Improvement District; Jamaica Performing Arts Center; Jamaica Station of the JFK AirTrain.

Kingsland Homestead (Queens Historical Society) & Bowne House

http://www.queenshistoricalsociety.org
http://www.bownehouse.org

Two historic houses are located within a block of one another in Flushing, Queens. The *Kingsland Homestead*, which serves as the home of the *Queens Historical Society*, was built between 1774 and 1785 and is located at the back of Weeping Beech Park. The *Bowne House*, built in 1661, is adjacent to the front of the park. The history that emanates from these two neighboring sites is rather remarkable, to say the least.

The *Kingsland Homestead* is one of the earliest surviving examples of the residential style construction on Long Island built in the late 18th Century. Captain Joseph King, a sea merchant and commercial farmer, bought this farmhouse, a Long Island half-house, from his father-in-law in1801. He named his new home *Kingsland* and the King family would live there until the 1930's. Captain King's daughter, Mary Ann, married Lindley Murray and their oldest daughter Mary was devoted to the cause of equality for African-Americans. In 1839, Captain King's son, Joseph, married the daughter of horticulturist James Bloodgood, owner of the Bloodgood Nursery. The nursery, one of the first on Long Island, would be run out of *Kingsland Homestead* for a time. The house, originally on Northern Boulevard, was moved a few hundred feet in 1926, as numbered streets and apartments began showing up. Declared a New York City Landmark in 1965, it was moved to its current location in 1968. In 1971, the *Queens Historical Society* opened in the *Kingsland Homestead* and remains there to this day.

The *Bowne House* was built by John Bowne in 1661, with additions added in 1669 and 1680. The footprint of the house today was completed in 1695. Bowne was dedicated to religious freedom and was arrested and deported to Holland in 1662 by New York Governor Peter Stuyvesant, when he defied the Governor's edict prohibiting the practice of religions other than the Dutch Reformed Church, by allowing a Quaker meeting in his house. Bowne then pled his case successfully to The Dutch West India Company, who ordered Stuyvesant to allow religious freedom. Bowne came home a hero in 1664 and today the precedent of religious freedom is embodied in *Bowne House*, which has been a museum since 1947. *Bowne House* is a New York City Landmark and is listed on the National Register of Historic Places. Both the *Bowne House* and the *Kingsland Homestead* have various educational programs.

From the final stop on the 7 train, Main Street, Flushing, also a stop for many buses, walk 2 blocks to Bowne Street and turn left. *Bowne House* is 2 blocks up and the *Queens Historical Society at the Kingsland Homestead* is located just past the Bowne House, in the back of Weeping Beech Park.

Walking Distance: Lewis H. Latimer House Museum; Main Street, Flushing.

.

Lewis H. Latimer House Museum

https://latimernow.org

The home of a pioneering figure currently resides in Flushing, Queens, to remind us that great accomplishments have nothing to do with background. The *Lewis H. Latimer House Museum* at 34-41 137th Street celebrates the life of a most relevant, yet often underappreciated African-American inventor, Lewis Howard Latimer. In his time, Latimer worked with many other inventors, including well known historical figures Alexander Graham Bell and Thomas Edison. In every stop along the way, he distinguished himself as an innovative thinker and well-respected man of science.

Born in 1848 in Chelsea, Massachusetts to a pair of former slaves, George and Rebecca Latimer, Lewis was the youngest of four children. He joined the Union Navy at age 16 in 1864 and was honorably discharged when the Civil War came to a close. From there, Latimer became an office boy for a patent law firm, Crosby & Gould, where he acquired tools used for sketching patent drawings. His supervisor recognized his raw talent and Latimer became a head draftsman by 1872. In 1876, he was chosen to assist Alexander Graham Bell and contributed to the drawings for Bell's telephone.

Latimer moved to Connecticut in 1879 and worked for Hiram Maxim, a rival of Thomas Edison's, until his job was inexplicably eliminated by Maxim while Latimer was in London working on the European production of Maxim's incandescent light. Undaunted, he went to work for the Edison Electric Light Company in 1884 and there he invented and patented the carbon filament, a significant improvement in the production of the incandescent light bulb. Latimer later supervised the installation of street lighting and the construction of electric plants in many American cities, as well as London and Montreal.

A painter and a poet as well, Latimer moved to Flushing, Queens in 1903 and lived there until his death at age 80 in 1928; his family owned the house until 1963. The *Latimer House*, including a tinkering lab that he added to the home (now used for many school projects), was moved from its original location on Holly Avenue to its current home on 137th Street and Leavitt Street, about a mile away. The *Lewis H. Latimer House Museum* allows visitors to touch base with one of America's greatest inventors, someone who just happened to be a black man.

To get to the *Lewis H. Latimer House Museum*, take the 7 train to the final stop, Main Street, Flushing. Walk four blocks down Main Street to Northern Boulevard, turn right and go three blocks to Leavitt Street. Turn left and walk straight ahead to the intersection at 137th Street. The Q25 bus to Linden Place and 35th Avenue leaves you two blocks away.

Walking Distance: Kingsland Manor/Queens Historical Society; Bowne House; Main Street, Flushing.

Louis Armstrong House Museum

http://louisarmstronghouse.org

An underappreciated site in New York City which I feel people really have to see is the *Louis Armstrong House Museum.* Located at 34-56 107th Street in Corona, Queens, this modest two-story brick building is a treasure trove of memories of one of the most famous musicians and performers of all-time, a man who despite his enormous fame, maintained a simple home life in a serene, tree-lined neighborhood. Though much smaller and understated than Elvis Presley's Memphis mansion, the *Louis Armstrong House Museum* is, to me, New York's answer to Graceland.

Lucille Armstrong bought the house in 1943 and immediately went about making a special home for her husband Louis, whom she had married a year before. By then, the great Satchmo was world famous and playing close to 300 gigs a year, so when he first arrived at his new home, he probably did not know how much it would mean to him, then 42-years old and having not yet had a genuine home base as an adult. From 1943 to 1971, when he died, that house in Queens became his "*Heaven on Earth*," as he saw it. With Lucille's meticulous decorating and the great trumpet player's foresight to leave behind a wealth of material that would one day fascinate visitors from all over, the *Louis Armstrong House Museum*, which opened in 2003 (twenty years after Lucille's death), is a most inspiring venue.

There is a Japanese garden which Lucille created and is still kept up on the property. While waiting to take one of the hourly guided tours of the house, guests are encouraged to sit out in the garden or go through the gift shop and welcoming center, which is cleverly housed where the garage used to be. After sifting through a room full of personal and professional Armstrong history and memorabilia in the welcome center, the tour begins with a five-minute video about the couple and the house. Inside the preserved home, which is just as it was in the 1960's, the Armstrong's last full decade together, audio prompts utilized in each room, taken from tapes that Louis recorded over the years, add texture to the wonder of being in the home of one of the world's truly transcendent artists. From the full-service kitchen to the master bedroom, two bathrooms and Louis' personal den, the home is fascinating and very familiar, if you happened to live in those times. The wallpapering in every room brings alive how so many homes looked in the 50's and 60's. Only this one was owned by a legend.

The 7 train to 103rd Street leaves you about 6 blocks from the *Louis Armstrong House Museum* on 34-56 107th Street, off 37th Avenue.

Walking Distance: Queens Museum; Hall of Science; Queens Zoo; U.S. Tennis Center; Tavern on the Green; Lemon Ice King of Corona; Citi Field.

Lower East Side Tenement Museum

http://www.tenement.org/contact.html

The most innovative venue in New York City is probably the *Lower East Side Tenement Museum.* Through a series of defined tours, the immigrant experience in New York is not just explained to, but experienced by all the visitors who happen by this most unnerving fork in the road. The *Tenement Museum* is an incredibly simple, yet brilliant concept, brought about through a well-preserved 19th Century building, where all the stories come to life.

Founded by social activists Ruth Abram and Anita Jacobson, the museum opened in 1992, when the first restored apartment of the museum's home, 97 Orchard Street, was completed. Since then, five more units have been revived in this tenement that had been abandoned for over 50 years at the time the *Tenement Museum* acquired the site. There are three types of tours utilized to tell the often gut-wrenching stories of immigrants of over a century ago. The research that went into shaping the *Tenement Museum* is impressive, as census records and other official documents from the late 1800's reveal the tales of people who actually lived in this most representative building.

There are three "*Meet the Residents*" tours, in which actors portray residents and inspectors of 97 Orchard Street and there are four "*Walk the Neighborhood*" tours, ranging from 1½ to 2 hours long. These social inspections help give the feel of how life in and around the neighborhood once was. They are both offered on selected dates, about once a month or so. But the real heart of the museum lies in the eight "*Tour the Building*" experiences, most available on a daily basis. These all take a particular family or aspect of life in a tenement and present it in a most visceral way. With titles like "*Shop Life,*" "*Irish Outsiders*" and "*Sweatshop Workers,*" these 1-1½ hour tours are very powerful, as you walk inside the reconstructed, yet still weathered homes of one-time tenants.

A few doors down from the *Tenement Museum*, at 103 Orchard Street, is a visitor's center with an astonishing book store that contains hundreds of titles referring to immigrant and tenement life. The various school programs offered at the *Tenement Museum* can truly shape young minds and plant the seeds of a social conscience. This is simply one of the best museums in *The City*.

The F train to Delancey Street and the J, N and Z trains to Essex Street all leave you two blocks from the *Lower East Side Tenement Museum* on Orchard Street. The B and D trains to Grand Street leave you about 6 blocks away. The B15 bus to Grand and Allen Streets leaves you one block from the museum.

Walking Distance: Chinatown; The Drawing Center; Museum of Chinese in America (MOCA); New Museum; Washington Square Park; S'Mac; The Basilica of Old St. Patrick's Cathedral; Museum at Eldridge Street; Tompkins Square Park; The Meatball Shop.

MoMA PS1

http://momaps1.org

One of the most visually-inspiring museums in *The City* is located in Long Island City, just one stop from Manhattan on the subway. Created inside of an old (1892-1963) public school, *MoMA PS1*, like its famous namesake, is a dedicated art museum, one that is enhanced by the site where it is housed.

MoMA PS1 was founded in 1971 by Alanna Heiss as the *Institute for Art and Urban Resources Inc.*, devoted to organizing exhibitions of contemporary artists in underutilized and abandoned spaces across New York City. After using various sites for five years, it presented its first landmark exhibit, *Rooms*, in 1976, at its current home at 22-25 Jackson Avenue. The unique open spaces available in the former public school contribute to *MoMA PS1* being an exhibition space rather than a collecting institution. *MoMA PS1* is one of the oldest and largest nonprofit contemporary art institutions in the United States. From 1976-96, known as the *P.S. 1 Contemporary Arts Center*, the building was used for studio, performance and exhibition spaces. In 1997, after renovations were done, the museum, by then called *MoMA PS1*, re-opened with its unique classroom-sized galleries intact. In 2000, the museum became an official affiliate of *The Museum of Modern Art.*

MoMA PS1 is a venue that needs to be seen. A school as the face of a museum is invigorating. The silhouette cut-outs which line a few of the staircases within scream *"Art!"* to the patrons. And then there is the permanent exhibit called "*Meeting*."

Artist James Turrell created *Skyspaces*, rooms that invited visitors to gaze into the sky above through an opening in the ceiling. "*Meeting*" was the second *Skyspace* that he completed and the first one in the United States. Commissioned in 1976, it was not realized until 1980 and was modified a few times before it opened to the public in 1986. In 2016, the seating was updated, with lighting added. As simple as it may seem, just sitting inside "*Meeting*," a small empty room with wooden seating all around and the sky above a very low ceiling is an absolute fabulous experience, unlike anything in *The City*.

A self-described "*artistic laboratory*," *MoMA PS1* presents concerts and other diverse activities. There is an eclectic bookshop, *ARTBOOK@MoMA PS1,* inside the museum, along with a small lunchroom-style restaurant called the *M. Wells Dinette*.

The E or the M trains to Court Square-23rd Street (Ely Avenue), the G to 21st Street-Van Alst and the 7 train to Court Square all leave you just a few blocks from *MoMA PS1* at 22-25 Jackson Avenue. The Q67 to Jackson and 46th Ave or the B62 to 46th Ave both strop right by *MoMA PS1*.

Walking Distance: Secret Theatre; Queens Plaza; 59th Street Bridge.

Mount Vernon Hotel Museum

http://www.mvhm.or

In the shadows of the 59th Street Bridge, there is a place where you can go back more than two centuries, to a time when the area we know as midtown was once considered the country. The *Mount Vernon Hotel Museum & Garden* is just that, a former hotel which now serves as a museum for the times it once lived in. Seemingly out of place amidst the whir of cars, trucks and foot traffic all around it, the *Mount Vernon*, located at 421 East 61st Street, is an absolute hidden-in-plain-sight jewel of *The City.*

As you walk down from First Avenue towards York Avenue, the over 200-year old structure suddenly sneaks up on you. Located at the top of a flight of weathered concrete stairs, the *Mount Vernon Hotel* still maintains the grand look that it did when it opened as a carriage house in 1799. From 1826-1833, the building was converted into a resort hotel, a preferred one for New Yorkers wanting to escape the "*City*" life which was then realized from 14th Street to the southern tip of Manhattan. Just a few blocks from a dock on the East River, which could deliver visitors by boat, the *Mount Vernon* also featured a regular schedule of stage coaches which went to and from downtown, from the hotel's entranceway. It was a so-called "*day hotel*," meaning guests did not stay overnight, but used it as a base for their daytime activities in the then countryside area. After it closed as a hotel, it was a residence until 1905, when it was purchased by the Standard Gas Light Company, now known as Con Edison. The Colonial Dames of America, a women's patriotic society, bought the building in 1924 and opened it as a museum in 1939.

The *Mount Vernon Hotel Museum* offers a 40-minute guided tour, which begins with a short video presentation that tells of the hotel's history, along with the region itself. After the film, a guide (in my case, Gloria, a wonderful 84-year young lady) takes you on a tour of the hotel, room-by-room. You learn how the men and women congregated in different areas of the establishment, with period-piece furniture and accoutrements weighing heavily on the historical nature of the *Mount Vernon*. There are group tours and other educational programs available at various times and a nice gift shop on the first floor.

The N, Q, R, 4, 5 and 6 trains to 59th Street/Lexington Avenue and the F train to Lexington Avenue/63rd Street all leave you a short walk from the *Mount Vernon Hotel Museum*. The M15, M31 or M57 buses all stop nearby, as well.

Walking Distance: Dangerfield's, Roosevelt Island Tramway; 59th Street Bridge

Museum at Eldridge Street

http://www.eldridgestreet.org

Sometimes you come across an old building in the middle of a neighborhood that has otherwise changed and the result usually leaves you in wonderment. The *Museum at Eldridge Street*, located just off Canal Street, is a place that aptly fits this description. The museum, a synagogue which was erected in 1887, was the first house of worship built in America by Eastern Europeans. At the time of its inception, it was part of the Five Points area, amidst immigrants of various backgrounds who lived in the surrounding tenements. In the course of time, the Italians, Polish, Russians, Jewish, Irish and others moved on. In the past half century or so, the neighborhood became known as Chinatown, as New York's growing Chinese community settled into the Canal Street area.

The *Eldridge Street Synagogue* flourished into the 1920's, but began to see a decline between the World Wars, as immigration restrictions and the Great Depression saw the main sanctuary used less and less. Following World War II, many congregants headed for the suburbs and those that remained had to settle for worshiping at the *Bes Midrah*, or house of study, on the synagogue's lower level, as the main sanctuary was not kept up and fell into disarray.

In the 1980's, a $20 million, 20-year restoration began and the resultant *Museum at Eldridge Street* is a fascinating and moving site to visit. The primary sanctuary contains storyboards and exhibits on the main and balcony levels, which describe nuances and traditions of a Jewish house of worship. To convert the originally 75 gas-powered lights in the main chandelier, the sockets were simply turned upside down to accommodate electric lighting. About 80% of the stained glass windows in the synagogue are original; five keyhole windows at the rear of the balcony represent the Five Books of the Torah. The *Ark,* or Holy Cabinet and the *Bimah,* or Reader's Platform, on the lower level, are very impressive and the actual footprints in the wooden floors at the back of the main sanctuary, where worshipers once stood for hours at a time in prayer, are almost beyond belief. A very informative ten-minute series of videos shown in a room just past the entrance is a great way to begin your visit, as a preview to all you will see. In 1996, the *Museum at Eldridge Street* was designated a National Historic Landmark.

The F to East Broadway, the B or the D to Grand Street and the J, N, Q, R and 6 trains to Canal Street all deliver you within walking distance of the *Museum at Eldridge Street.* The M15 bus to Grand and Allen Streets also leaves you just a short walk away.

Walking Distance: Chinatown; The Drawing Center; Museum of Chinese in America (MOCA); New Museum; The Basilica of Old St. Patrick's Cathedral; Lower East Side Tenement Museum.

Museum of American Finance

http://www.moaf.org/index

Some museums are found exactly where they should be, or certainly where one would imagine them to be. One such venue is the *Museum of American Finance*, located right in the midst of New York's financial district. It is situated on the site of the original Bank of New York, which opened in 1796 as New York's first bank. The current building opened in 1929 and also served as a Bank of New York, into the 1990's. That one day this site might become the home of a museum dedicated to finance wasn't such a stretch.

Originally the result of a pair of exhibits at Bowling Green, the *Museum of American Finance* was housed at 24 Broadway (in 1992) and then 28 Broadway (in 1996), before moving into its current home at 48 Wall Street in 2008. Most of the exhibits, all located on the second floor of the museum, speak of the evolution of money, trading and financial theories and practices in the history of the United States. There are a number of stocks, bonds and other forms of currency on display throughout the site. The birth and growth of the *Wall Street Journal* is touched upon and various items and machinery used in the stock market through the years, such as ticker tape, are also on display.

One of the most compelling exhibits is the *Alexander Hamilton Room,* which contains artifacts pertaining to the first Secretary of the Treasury of the United States, who was also one of the men who'd opened the Bank of New York on this very site in 1796. Quotes from Hamilton line the walls, documents he authored are showcased and a set of pistols replicates the ones used by Hamilton and Aaron Burr in the most famous duel in history. If the *Hamilton Room* isn't the most interesting part of the museum, the room containing *Money; A History*, probably is. Here you'll find actual Confederate currency, plus notes and images of seldom seen bills and the men who adorn them, such as the $500 (William McKinley), the $1,000 (Grover Cleveland), the $10,000 (Salmon Chase) and the $100,000 (Woodrow Wilson).

The darker side of money is shown in a kiosk that chronicles stage coach, train and bank robbers, such as Jesse James, Butch Cassidy, John Dillinger and Willie Sutton. The gift shop on the first floor offers the type of unique items that you'd imagine such a singularly pointed museum would.

The 2, 3, 4 and 5 trains to Wall Street leave you a few blocks from the *Museum of American Finance*. The J train to Broad Street does the same. The M1, M6, M9 and M15 buses stop right nearby.

Walking Distance: Federal Hall; South Street Seaport District; Pier 6 Helicopter Tours; 9/11 Memorial & Museum; Skyscraper Museum; Museum of Jewish Heritage; National Museum of the American Indian; Battery Park; Canyon of Heroes; Statue of Liberty/Ellis Island Ferries; Staten Island Ferry.

Museum of Chinese in America (MOCA)

http://www.mocanyc.org

The Canal Street neighborhood known as Chinatown mirrors other such enclaves that have sprung up in other American cities, though along with San Francisco's version, New York's Chinatown is one of the two most famous in the country. At 215 Centre Street, just off Canal, there sits a small museum which tells the tale of how Chinese immigrants became Chinese Americans. The *Museum of Chinese in America (MOCA)* contains a plethora of items which help to explain how Chinatown came to be, in New York City and beyond.

Founded in 1980, the *Museum of Chinese in America* began as a community-based organization. Historian John Kuo Wei Tchen and community resident/activist Charles Lai's New York Chinatown History Project would lead to *MOCA*, which was created to develop a better understanding of Chinese American history and community. The concern that the memories and experiences of aging older generations would be lost was also a factor in the birth of *MOCA*. Essentially preserving and presenting the history, heritage and culture of people of Chinese descent in the United States was the mandate. The diverse experiences of Chinese Americans as they attempted to fit into their new home is a central theme at *MOCA*, where interactive exhibits are featured throughout. Citing 160 years of Chinese American history, the museum features a number of profile plates, spread all around the venue, which celebrate various Chinese Americans of note, ranging from architect I.M. Pei to martial arts champion and actor Bruce Lee to Olympic Gold Medal figure skater Michelle Kwan.

The cultural place occupied through the years by Chinese Americans is illustrated in exhibits which feature early moving pictures, the preponderance of laundries run by the Chinese and even the rise of gangs in the 1970's. The significance of art and food in the story of the Chinese in America and the historic timeline, which poses thought-provoking questions like "*Where Does Chinatown End*?" are noteworthy. After over 30 years of collecting artifacts, the *Museum of Chinese in America* also maintains its original site at 70 Mulberry Street as a Collections and Research Center. As it is, *MOCA* owns the largest Chinese American collection in the United States, featuring over 65,000 artifacts, including oral histories, textiles and photographs. Additionally, there are various educational programs for children, adults and seniors. All things considered, *MOCA* is both interesting and unique and a most informative stop on the road.

If you take the A, C, E, J, N, Q, R, 1 or 6 trains to any of their Canal Street stops, you will be just a short walk from 215 Centre Street, where the *Museum of Chinese in America* is located.

Walking Distance: Chinatown; Museum at Eldridge Street; The Drawing Center; New Museum; The Basilica of Old St. Patrick's Cathedral; Lower East Side Tenement Museum.

Museum of Mathematics (MoMath)

http://momath.org

One of the newest theme museums in New York City is the *Museum of Mathematics,* or *MoMath*, which is located at 11 east 26th Street in the Flatiron district. Chartered on November 17, 2009 and opening in 2012, *MoMath* is a most unique museum and learning center. Officially known as *The National Museum of Mathematics*, it began in response to the closing of a small museum of mathematics on Long Island, the Goudreau Museum. An inspired group with a love and interest in math quickly discovered that there was now no museum of mathematics in the United States; *MoMath* was their answer to this apparent problem.

Of all New York museums, the *Museum of Mathematics* most closely resembles the Hall of Science in Flushing Meadows Park, in that the two floors of the museum contain a plethora of exhibits which are interactive and experimental. This makes *MoMath* a most wonderful venue to take children and young adults, as properties of mathematics are on display all around you. They cleverly call the main floor Level Zero (0) and the basement level Negative One (-1). This only enhances the most striking aspect of *MoMath*, which is that it is simply fun. Whether you are an adult or a child, while trying one of the experiments or watching others do so, the place oozes a joy that should be savored. *MoMath* is one of the most purely fun places to have arrived on *The City* landscape in recent times.

The museum allows the visitor to see math in action, through various exhibits which center on math-inspired items, such as optics and light, the power of shapes, art and science. There are a number of continuing programs, such as "*Math Encounters*" and "*Composite Chat*," which encourage all who are interested in math to attend. A full list of upcoming events can be found on their website. A most eclectic gift shop, filled with t-shirts, games, books, toys and other crafts with a math bend to them is located to the left of the entrance. All in all, a visit to the *National Museum of Mathematics* offers one an enjoyable ride unlike any in *The City*, save the aforementioned Hall of Science.

The F or M trains to 23rd Street and the N, R or 6 trains to either 23rd or 28th Streets all leave you a few blocks from the *Museum of Mathematics*. The M1 and M3 buses to Fifth Avenue and West 26th Street, the M2 to Madison and East 27th Street and the M23 bus to East 23rd Street/Broadway all leave you just a few blocks away from *MoMath*.

Walking Distance: Flatiron Building; Madison Square Park; Theodore Roosevelt Birthplace; The High Line; Union Square Park; Old Town Bar and Restaurant; Irish Repertory Theatre.

National Jazz Museum in Harlem

http://jazzmuseuminharlem.org

Some institutions really cry out for a museum, especially in certain areas where those industries thrived. One such venue in New York City is the *National Jazz Museum in Harlem*, located on the first floor of 58 West 129th Street, just off Lenox Avenue.

Jazz music, one of the truly unique American creations, is still revered today, in various clubs in Greenwich Village and the popular *Jazz at Lincoln Center* program, moderated by the great Wynton Marsalis. But it is uptown, in Harlem, where the art form first thrived in New York and continues to do so today. Jazz has been a huge part of the scene since the 1920's Harlem Renaissance. For decades, legendary names like Duke Ellington, Louis Armstrong, Ella Fitzgerald and Billie Holiday shared the joy of jazz in classic venues like the Savoy Ballroom and the Apollo Theater. The memories of these and other great masters of jazz really deserved a space to try and spread the story of this most affecting musical style.

In 1997, jazz in New York came home, when the *National Jazz Museum in Harlem* was founded by Leonard Garment and Abraham D. Sofaer. The museum spent 15 years located in East Harlem, before moving to its current space in Central Harlem in 2015. The stated goal of the *National Jazz Museum is Harlem* is to promote and present jazz by spreading awareness on local, national and international levels. The museum itself is modest, just a studio-sized room, with a number of interesting artifacts, including vintage instruments used by various artists. There are a few listening areas, where one can hear, among other things, a session with Duke Ellington's band. Revered Harlem-based jazz pianists and composers, James P. Johnson, Fats Waller and Willie 'The Lion" Smith are recognized and a giant cut-out of Dizzy Gillespie greets you at the front door. The museum proper is a good starting point to the related programs at the core of what the *Jazz Museum* is all about.

There are about 80 free programs a year originating at the museum, with hundreds of professional jazz artists participating. The museum presents a continuous line-up of live performances, exhibitions and educational programs and is home to the Savory Collection, more than 100 hours of live recordings by jazz legends made in New York City between 1935 and 1941. Going forward, an even larger home base is part of the vision.

The *National Jazz Museum in Harlem* is within walking distance of the 125th Street station of the 2 or 3 trains and just a few more blocks from the A, B, C, D or 1 trains. The M2, M7, M10, M100, M101, M102 and BX 15 buses all stop nearby.

Walking Distance: Apollo Theatre; 125th Street Business Improvement District; Studio Museum in Harlem; Schomburg Center

National Lighthouse Museum

http://lighthousemuseum.org

A relatively new museum located just outside the Staten Island Ferry terminal, the *National Lighthouse Museum* is a very intriguing venue. This nautical history building at the former site (1862-1965) of the U.S. Lighthouse Service (USLHS) General Depot at St. George, Staten Island, was selected from amongst 17 deserving proposals to be the home of the *National Lighthouse Museum.* The American Lighthouse Coordinating Committee (ALCC), whose mandate was to find a home for the museum, cited the historic significance of the location at St. George, as well as the high volume of visitors who passed through the ferry terminal, in making their decision.

The first signs of concern for lighthouses came in 1948, when the Shinnecock Light, on the south shore of Long Island, became unstable and was demolished and eventually replaced by a golf course, to the chagrin of many locals who made unsuccessful efforts to save the structure. Decades passed, but by 1982, concerns that other classic lighthouses would go the way of Shinnecock led to the formation of the Lighthouse Preservation Society (LPS), a national organization based in Rockport, Massachusetts. The LPS strove to educate and preserve the navigational history of lighthouses, which were becoming obsolete, due to new technologies, like solar panels and later GPS's. The movement trudged along until the 1990's, when the famous Fire Island Light was being targeted for destruction. The real threat to this lighthouse and other landmark lighthouses around the country led to the formation of the ALCC. A charter was given for the *National Lighthouse Museum* on November 9, 2001 and the museum opened on August 7, 2015.

The current site of the *National Lighthouse Museum* was also, from 1799 to the mid-1850's, the location of the New York Marine Hospital, also known as *The Quarantine*, a group of buildings which pre-dated Ellis Island as a processing center for immigrants. The *National Lighthouse Museum*, housed in Building #11, contains some wonderful exhibits, including a Historic Lighthouse Timeline, a collection of lighthouse miniatures and an informative display, the History of Lighthouse Keepers. Building #10, a much larger space right next door, will be the museum's permanent home in a few years, following renovations, which will make this truly fascinating historical museum about four times the size of what it is today.

The 1 train to South Ferry, the 4 and 5 to Bowling Green and the R and W to Whitehall Street/South Ferry all leave you by the Manhattan entrance to the Staten Island Ferry. After disembarking from the ferry at the St. George Terminal in Staten Island, you follow signs to the *National Lighthouse Museum*, which is located to the left of the ferry terminal.

Walking Distance: St. George Theatre; Staten Island Ferry Terminal; Richmond County Bank Ballpark (Staten Island Yankees); Staten Island Museum in St. George.

Neue Galerie New York

http://www.neuegalerie.org

A particularly polished and impressive museum, the *Neue Galerie New York*, on the corner of 86th Street and Fifth Avenue, is also notable for the briskly moving line outside waiting to get in. A museum of German and Austrian art, the *Neue Galerie New York* aspires to share a particular time and place with those of a mind to explore.

The *Neue Galerie* (which does indeed mean "new gallery") takes its name from different European galleries of the past, most notably the *Neue Galerie in Vienna.* The site at 1048 Fifth Avenue consists of three floors which display a far-ranging collection of early 20th Century German and Austrian art and design. The Austrian collection contains a number of large portraits, which dominate a few walls in the *Neue Galerie.* The German collection seems a bit more adventurous, as there are a fair amount of pencil and charcoal drawings, which contrast very nicely with pieces of furniture from the Era, including a large 100-year old men's wardrobe closet, which is remarkably preserved. Beyond the permanent German and Austrian art that is at the centerpiece of the museum's collection, there are rotating exhibitions mixed in on the third floor. The *Neue Galerie New York* has an intangible quality about it, one that might be attributed to the building that houses it and the two determined men who bought that building to share their collective vision.

Serge Sabarsky was an art dealer and a museum organizer. He became friends with Ronald S. Lauder, an art collector and philanthropist. Over three decades, their shared love for Modern German and Austrian art brought them closer to their goal of opening a museum that would house such items. As for the building at 1048 Fifth Avenue, it was completed in 1914 by the same architects who erected the New York Public Library. Mrs. Cornelius Vanderbilt III, a noted socialite, once called it home and it was eventually granted landmark status by the New York Landmarks Commission. Sabarsky and Lauder bought the building in 1994, though Sabarsky passed away in 1996, before they could launch their museum. Lauder carried on and opened the *Neue Galerie New York* in November of 2001.

Upon approaching the museum, one will generally find a line outside. This is because they have a security metal detector immediately inside the door, so they have to filter people in, about 4-5 at a time. The wait is never long. Once inside, a winding staircase leads you to the exhibit floors. It is a very professionally run museum, with a pair of cafes on the premises, too.

The 6 train to 86th Street station leaves you just a few blocks from the *Neue Galerie*.

Walking Distance: Cooper Hewitt; National Academy; Solomon R. Guggenheim Museum; Jewish Museum; Metropolitan Museum of Art; Central Park Great Lawn; Marx Brothers Place & Playground.

New Museum

http://www.newmuseum.org

Founded in 1977 and in its current location at 235 Bowery since December of 2007, the *New Museum* arrived as the only museum in Manhattan devoted exclusively to contemporary art and is one of the leading contemporary art museums in the world. In the earliest years, the *New Museum* took a unique place at a crossroads between an alternative venue and a respected major space which could be embraced by a most broad range of patrons, be they lovers of diversity or disciples of historical value.

Founding Director Marcia Tucker had been a curator at the *Whitney Museum of American Art* from 1967-76. At *The Whitney*, she had an inside look at how new work by living artists was not easily factored into the usual type of exhibitions that most traditional art museums leaned toward. To be recognized alongside older, established artists and artworks was not something Tucker saw happening in the conventional art museums. This led her to envisioning an institution devoted to the presentation, interpretation and study of contemporary art. She officially founded the *New Museum* on January 1, 1977 and the first exhibition, entitled "*Memory*," was organized by Tucker at *C Space*, an alternative spot near the museum's temporary offices on Hudson Street in Tribeca. The exhibition reflected on connections between personal and collective memory and like every *New Museum* exhibition that followed, it was accompanied by a catalogue which documented the exhibition for present and future audiences.

In 1977, the *New Museum* moved to a small gallery and office located at the New School for Social Research at 65 Fifth Avenue, at 14th Street. In 1983, Board President Henry Luce III negotiated a long-term lease for the *New Museum* in the Astor Building in SoHo at 583 Broadway, between Houston and Prince Streets. This site had much larger gallery spaces and offices, and, after a major renovation in 1997, a bookstore was added, with an international selection of publications on art, theory, and culture at large.

In 1996, the museum began to focus increasingly on solo exhibitions by significant international artists who had not yet received attention in the U. S., including Mona Hatoum (1998), William Kentridge (2001) and Marlene Dumas (2002). On December 1, 2007, the *New Museum* re-opened at 235 Bowery with facilities that included a theater, five floors of gallery spaces and a distinctive Sky Room with wonderful panoramic views of lower Manhattan. The simple mission statement of the *New Museum*, "*New Art, New Ideas*" sums up a most enjoyable venue that should thrive well into the 21st Century.

The N and R trains to Prince Street and the 6 train to Spring Street all leave you within walking distance of the *New Museum.*

Walking Distance: Lower East Side Tenement Museum; Museum at Eldridge Street; Museum of Chinese in America; The Drawing Center; Tompkins Square Park; The Basilica of Old St. Patrick's Cathedral; Ukrainian Museum; The Meatball Shop; Washington Square Park.

Nicholas Roerich Museum

http://www.roerich.org

A really interesting museum dedicated to the works of a single artist, the *Nicholas Roerich Museum*, located on 107th Street off Broadway, offers New Yorkers a most impressive collection. Nicholas Roerich was a noted Russian-born artist, writer, humanitarian and philosopher. The *Nicholas Roerich Museum* has 150 of his paintings on display in its permanent collection. This site provides one of the truly enjoyable art museums in New York City, due to its pointed focus and defined goal to show the world the level of achievement that this remarkable individual left behind.

Nicholas Roerich was born in St. Petersburg, Russia, in 1874. He found a natural love and aptitude for sketching as a young boy, but his father, Konstantin, a lawyer, thought that being an artist served little purpose to society. When Nicholas reached college age, the two compromised and Roerich went to both law and art school in St. Petersburg. After writing his college thesis, Roerich embarked on a lifetime dedicated to the arts. He became a fine theatrical set designer, a poet of note and a prolific painter. Along with his wife Helena, who was an accomplished pianist and writer herself, they formed the *Agni Yoga Society*, which spoke to the philosophies and religious teachings of all ages. During their adult lives together, they spent time in Finland, New York, India and throughout Europe, displaying Nicholas' paintings, while teaching and writing a number of books apiece. A champion of human rights, Roerich was nominated for the Nobel Peace Prize three times.

In New York in 1921, Roerich founded the *Master Institute of United Arts*, which flourished until 1937. The institute was reborn in 1949 as the *Nicholas Roerich Museum*, located in the brownstone where it still resides today. Many of the works currently on display are from the original 1949 collection. Roerich lived in India for a time and the Himalayan Mountains that his family settled near formed the subject of many of the paintings on display in the *Nicholas Roerich Museum.* He also painted a number of religious images and referenced the growing role of women as he saw it in other works. As a bonus, there are two paintings of Roerich himself, done by his son, Svetoslav, as well as a small collection of Roerich's books. There are also classical concerts held on site regularly. If this very polished collection is any indication, I would surely love to see other museums dedicated to the works of one particular artist.

The 1 train to 110th Street leaves you three blocks from the *Nicholas Roerich Museum.* The M104 bus to 108th Street and Broadway and the M5 bus to 108th Street and Riverside Drive both leave you a block away.

Walking Distance: Riverside Park; Columbia University; Riverside Church; General Grant National Memorial; Central Park North.

Noguchi Museum & Socrates Sculpture Park

http://www.noguchi.org

On the banks of the East River in Long Island City, there is a most creative little pocket of land, highlighted by a wonderful museum dedicated to the work of a 20th Century master and a brow-beaten park which serves as an outdoor exhibit space for large scale sculptures, which would do the namesake of the museum a block away proud. The *Noguchi Museum* offers up a solid array of abstract art and the *Socrates Sculpture Park*, when exhibits are on site, compliments the *Noguchi Museum* quite well.

Isamu Noguchi (1904–1988), born of a Japanese father who abandoned him and his mother and an American mother who couldn't always cope, spent his life traversing between his two ethnic backgrounds. He was one of the twentieth century's most critically acclaimed sculptors, who also created gardens, furniture and lighting designs, ceramics, architecture, and set designs. Born in Los Angeles, California, Noguchi lived in Japan until he was thirteen, when he moved to Indiana. This began a lifelong quest around the world, with his most extensive successes occurring in Japan, the United States and Mexico. Among his most celebrated triumphs was a 1946 delicate-slab sculptures exhibit called "*Fourteen Americans*," which ran to rave reviews at the Museum of Modern Art (MoMA) in New York. As a New Yorker who was not cited for imprisonment, he famously volunteered to join the forced internment camps for Japanese-Americans in Arizona, following the Pearl Harbor attack of 1941. He stayed in the camp for seven months, before returning to New York, where he opened a studio in Greenwich Village.

In 1985, Noguchi opened the *Isamu Noguchi Garden Museum* (now known as the *Noguchi Museum*), in Long Island City, New York. This museum, designed by Noguchi himself, marked the culmination of his commitment to public spaces. Located in a 1920's industrial building across the street from where the artist had established a studio in 1960, this recently renovated structure today features two floors or winding galleries of his sculptures, which are connected by ramps and staircases to an impressive garden gallery. There is also a documentary about Noguchi's life constantly playing in one corner of the second floor.

The *Socrates Sculpture Park*, a block down from the *Noguchi Museum*, is a dusky yard right on the East River which has exhibitions a few times a year, while otherwise serving as a contemplative spot and dog-walking area.

The N and W trains to the Broadway station in Astoria/Long Island City leave you a short walk west to the *Socrates Sculpture Park* on Broadway and Vernon Boulevard and the *Noguchi Museum* on 9-01 33rd Road, off Vernon Boulevard. The Q103 and Q104 buses stop near both sites.

Walking Distance: Roosevelt Island; Queensbridge Park; Queens Plaza; 59th Street Bridge; Athens Square Park.

Old Stone House at Washington Park

http://theoldstonehouse.org

One of the more curiously positioned historic houses that have been preserved in New York City is the *Old Stone House*, located in Washington Park, on the border of Park Slope and Gowanus. The farmhouse, built in 1699, found itself in the middle of American history on more than one occasion.

The Battle of Brooklyn was the first military engagement following the adoption of the Declaration of Independence in July, 1776. On the morning of August 27th, 1776, the British, under General William Howe, defeated the undermanned Patriot forces. The *Old Stone House* served as a fortress in this battle. The Patriots suffered over 1,000 casualties, while the British lost around 400. The British proceeded to occupy Brooklyn, though General George Washington and his army did escape across the East River, due to the valor of General William Alexander's Patriot militia, known as the *Maryland 400*, who valiantly held off Howe's redcoats at the *Old Stone House* long enough for Washington's forces to retreat and regroup.

A fortress from the Revolutionary War that survived would be fascinating enough, but the *Old Stone House* crossed paths with history again in the 1880's. When the Brooklyn Base Ball Club (not yet called the Trolley Dodgers) began playing at the original Washington Park (from 1883-1891), the *Old Stone House*, located on the grounds, became the team's clubhouse. In 1891, the team moved a few miles away, to Eastern Park, before returning in 1898 under their new owner, Charlie Ebbets, to a second Washington Park, built a block away from the original. The Trolley Dodgers/Superbas would play in this Washington Park until 1912, before moving into fabled Ebbets Field in 1913. The *Old Stone House* is all that survives from the original Washington Park. A brick wall on Third Avenue and First Street is all that remains of the second Washington Park.

In August of 1935, on the site of the original Washington Park, the J.J. Byrne Playground was born, one of over 200 children's areas opening that year as part of a playground construction program. The *Old Stone House* was repaired and today, along with the Byrne Playground and a turf field, collectively constitutes the current Washington Park. The *Old Stone House* is open Friday to Sunday, while the sounds of children's laughter pierce the air around the playground in front of it, as well as the playing field behind it.

The R train to 9th Street and the F train to Fourth Avenue both leave you a few blocks from the *Old Stone House*, which is between Third and Fourth Streets, bordered by Fourth and Fifth Avenues. The B63 bus stops at Fifth Avenue and Third Street, just down the block.

Walking Distance: Barclay's Center; Brooklyn Academy of Music (BAM).

Park Avenue Armory

http://www.armoryonpark.org

One of the most impressive buildings in all of New York City is the *Park Avenue Armory*, located between 66th and 67th streets on that most storied city thoroughfare. Originally built for the Seventh regiment in 1880, the *Armory* today is the home of some of *The City's* best alternate artistic presentations. The efforts of preservationist Wade Thompson to restore the *Armory* were so profound that the building is now actually called the *Thompson Art Center at Park Avenue Armory*. The 55,000 square foot *Wade Thompson Drill Hall* is constantly being arranged and re-arranged to satisfy the needs of the *Armory's* particular presentation du jour.

The *Armory's* exterior was built using the guide of many buildings on Fifth Avenue in the late 1800's, with some of the interior rooms designed by such architectural luminaries as Stanford White and Louis Comfort Tiffany. Though it was a military institution, the site was always more of a social club for the members of the Seventh Regiment of the National Guard, the first volunteer unit to respond to Abraham Lincoln's call to arms in 1861. The drill hall was used more for parties and presentations than for actual drilling, even in its earliest days. The Veterans Room on the first floor was hailed as one of the most magnificently crafted rooms in all of New York, with its touches of Islamic, Chinese, Greek, Celtic, Egyptian and Persian architecture. Long after the Seventh Regiment used the *Park Avenue Armory* as its home, the building stood without alterations. The majestic interiors were used in the 1983 Dan Aykroyd/Eddie Murphy comedy *Trading Places*. But by the late 1990's, the neglected structure was falling into disrepair.

In 2000, the *Armory* found itself on the World Monuments Fund's list of the "*100 Most Endangered Historic Sites in the World*." Help arrived in 2007, when Wade Thompson and the *Park Avenue Armory*

Conservancy began turning the *Armory* into an alternate artistic home, through massive renovations which continue to this day. Thompson died in 2009, but the *Conservancy* continues to steer the venue in the 21st Century. The drill hall is the largest open space in *The City* being used for artistic presentations. The Veterans Room has been fully renovated, as has the former Board of Officers Room, which is now used for recitals and smaller performances. Large paintings of former Seventh Regiment alumni hang throughout the *Armory*, which holds private tours that I would highly recommended.

The F train to 63rd and Lexington Avenue and the 6 train to 68th Street/Hunter College leave you a few blocks from the *Park Avenue Armory* on 643 Park Avenue. The 59th Street/Lexington Avenue station (N, R, Q and W trains) is also nearby.

Walking Distance: Roosevelt House; Central Park Zoo; Museum of American Illustration; The Frick Collection; Asia Society.

Poe Cottage & Park

http://bronxhistoricalsociety.org/poe-cottage

Of all the places around *The City* that I have gone to in my life, particularly in the last five years, the *Edgar Allan Poe Cottage* on East Kingsbridge Road and Grand Concourse and the adjacent *Poe Park* is easily one of my favorites. Being a huge fan of the father of the modern detective story might factor into that equation, but I think the fact that the cottage was the final home of one of the greatest American writers is more at the core of my sensibilities.

Built in 1812, Poe moved into the cottage in 1846 with his wife, Virginia and her mother, Mrs. Maria Clemm. At the time, the area known as Fordham was countryside and Poe moved there for the fresh air that he thought would help his wife's tuberculosis. Unfortunately, Virginia died in 1847, but Poe and his mother-in-law continued to live there until Poe died in Baltimore during a speaking tour in 1849. Mrs. Clemm moved out upon Poe's death and the cottage was rented out for decades, until the City of New York bought the property, moved it a block to avoid possible demolition and made it into a museum in 1913.

Inside the cottage museum, the over 200-year old structure is amazingly fit, though the sloping ceilings in some rooms require that you duck down to go inside. The Bronx Historical Society offers informative guides throughout the day, from Thursday through Sunday. Most of the furniture is comprised of period pieces, but a rocking chair and the bed that Virginia Poe died in are from the original structure. A small lodging, the *Poe Cottage* is very intriguing, with a bust and a few portraits of the writer adding to the atmosphere. The master bedroom on the second floor is now used for screening a 17-minute film on the history of the cottage and Poe himself.

A visitors' center adjacent to the cottage is located within the appropriately named *Poe Park*, which features a kids' play area and an old gazebo waiting for some instruments to arrive. The *Poe Cottage* welcomes groups and there are regular events in *Poe Park*, as well as the visitors' center. *Poe Cottage*, where one of the greatest American writers created some of his impressive catalog, including one of his most famous poems, "*Annabel Lee*," is a New York City and State landmark and is on the Register of Historic Places.

The D train to Kingsbridge Road leaves you right across the street from the *Poe Cottage*. The Kingsbridge Road stop on the 4 train is about 5 blocks away. The Bx1, Bx2, Bx28, and BxM4 buses all have stops right by *Poe Cottage*.

Walking Distance: St. James Park & Tennis Courts; Lehman Center for the Performing Arts.

Roosevelt House

http://www.roosevelthouse.hunter.cuny.edu/visitor-information

Sara Delano Roosevelt's gift of a home to her son, Franklin and his new bride, Eleanor, would become a very significant part of American history. Today, the *Roosevelt House*, located at 47-49 East 65th Street, between Park and Madison Avenues, provides an enlightened look back to a time a century ago, when the future 32nd President and his extremely socially active wife laid the foundation for their most transcendent lives.

In 1905, Sara Roosevelt gave Franklin and Eleanor a Christmas card with a rough sketch she drew of a house that she was commissioning for them in Manhattan. Completed in 1908, the Roosevelts moved in, Sara into 47 East 65th Street and Franklin, Eleanor and their two young children, Anna and James, into the adjoining number 49. For a quarter of a century, the couple would call the town house home and during that time, it was the central headquarters for FDR's rising political career and Eleanor's public presence as a resounding voice for human rights. The house was also a behind-the-scenes rehab center, following Franklin's devastating 1921 bout with polio. At the *Roosevelt House*, he painstakingly practiced walking with braces and developing techniques to cloak his affliction, such as leaning onto rails and having someone, usually his son James, right by his side, with an arm on him for support. The path from New York State Senator to U.S. Assistant Secretary of the Navy to Governor of New York was navigated in FDR's personal library, where, with his core advisors, like Frances Perkins, he held countless strategy and policy meetings. After being elected President in November of 1932, the Roosevelts left behind mother Sara and this most electric breeding ground. All this is relived today in wonderfully guided tours of the *Roosevelt House*.

Following a full renovation in 2010, the *Roosevelt House* opened to the public, while also serving as a space of learning for its owner, Hunter College, which acquired the building after Sara died in 1941. The Saturday tours are notable for their presentation, as large screen kiosks located in different rooms help tell the story of the *Roosevelt House*, through pictures and videos. There are photos of the times throughout the house, makeshift classrooms and even a small theater on the lower floor, all of which speak to the spirit of learning and history that Hunter College so successfully presents to both visitors and students.

The F train to 63rd and Lexington Avenue leaves you a few blocks from the *Roosevelt House* at 47-49 East 65th Street, as does the 6 train to 68th Street/Hunter College. The N, R, Q and W trains to 59th Street/ Lexington Avenue are a few blocks further away, but well within walking distance.

Walking Distance: Central Park Zoo; Museum of American Illustration; The Frick Collection; Park Avenue Armory; Asia Society.

Staten Island Museum

http://www.statenislandmuseum.org

The *Staten Island Museum*, the oldest cultural center in Staten Island, now has three locations. The original building at 75 Stuyvesant Place, just off the Staten Island Ferry terminal, is now complemented by two buildings in Snug Harbor, at 1000 Richmond Terrace, a short bus ride from the ferry. Inside the historic Snug Harbor Cultural Center and Botanical Garden, the *Staten Island Museum History Center & Archives* was added in 2009 (Building H) and directly adjacent from that structure stands what is now the flagship location of the museum franchise, the *Staten Island Museum at Snug Harbor*, which arrived in 2015 (Building A).

The root of the idea for the *Staten Island Museum* came in 1881, when 14 young naturalists on Staten Island thought to combine their collections and research efforts. Determined to record natural life for future generations, they became environmental preservationists long before that was something regularly advocated by any person or group. Today, that effect can be vibrantly seen in the detailed exhibits featuring hordes of natural life. Butterflies, insects, birds, fossils and the like are displayed meticulously in an area called the Hall of Natural Sciences. Other traveling exhibits in St. George and Snug Harbor give a nod to the museums' origins as a naturalist's dream. But there is also another story that shapes the *Staten Island Museum* today.

The fame of the Staten Island Ferry and the island which it is named after has given the area a wonderful maritime history. This can be experienced through exhibits featuring artifacts from the various classes of ferries that have been utilized through the years, as well as a timeline of the history of the Staten Island Ferry itself. With renovations underway at St. George, the ultimate goal in the next decade or so is to house the natural collections in Snug Harbor, along with exhibits about the history of Staten Island, while presenting the maritime landscape at the St. George building, right near the ferry terminal. There are school programs and a group bird watch as part of the museum's yearly agenda.

The 1 train to South Ferry, the 4 and 5 to Bowling Green and the R and W to Whitehall Street/South Ferry all leave you by the Manhattan entrance to the Staten Island Ferry. From the St. George Ferry Terminal, you go to the right, following signs to the Richmond County Ballpark. Turn left and walk up the ramp beside the ballpark to Richmond Terrace. The *Staten Island Museum* at St. George is one block from the ballpark, at 75 Stuyvesant Place. To get to the Snug Harbor branches of the museum, you take the S40 bus from the ferry terminal to the Snug Harbor stop.

Walking Distance: St. George: St. George Theatre; Staten Island Ferry Terminal; Richmond County Bank Ballpark (Staten Island Yankees); National Lighthouse Museum. Snug Harbor: New York Chinese Scholar's Garden; Allison Park.

Steinway Mansion

http://friendsofsteinwaymansion.org

There are a number of historic houses that have been designated National and/or New York City Landmarks, which are now operated as museums, learning centers or party venues. Unfortunately, there are others which have not been transformed as yet, though they remain fairly intact and awaiting a new birth, of sorts. One of the most prominent of these structures is the *Steinway Mansion* in the northernmost section of Astoria, Queens.

What would become the *Steinway Mansion* was built in 1858 by Benjamin Pike, Jr., a noted manufacturer of scientific instruments produced in lower Manhattan. Pike died in 1864 and his widow sold the property in 1870 to piano maker William Steinway, one of three sons of Steinway & Sons founder Henry E. Steinway. The huge home became known as the *Steinway Mansion*, from then on. The Steinway family, including William and his brothers Charles and Henry, had come to the United States from Germany in 1850. They founded the firm of Steinway & Sons in 1853. In short order, the Steinway name became omnipresent in Astoria, as they pretty much built a small city, the Steinway Village, which featured a musical performance venue (Steinway Hall), a Steinway Concert & Artist department and a Steinway Piano Factory, all on land that was owned by the family. Near the piano factory, there was housing for Steinway workers, a church, a library and a kindergarten, as well as a public trolley line. The *Steinway Mansion* and the piano factory (a few blocks away) are all that still stands today.

Jack Halberian purchased the *Steinway Mansion* in 1926 and when he died in 1976, his son Michael began an extensive restoration. The house, on sale since 2010, when Michael Halberian died, was purchased by two anonymous buyers for $2.6 million in May of 2014. The *Steinway Mansion* was landmarked by the City of New York in

1966 and it was listed on the National Register of Historic Places in 1983. In recent times, a group called *The Friends of the Steinway Mansion* formed, with the goal of trying to get the house refurbished and opened as a museum or a learning center. How the new owners and *The Friends of the Steinway Mansion* interact will doubtless determine what the next step will be for the *Steinway Mansion*. Until then, you can still go up on the hill where the impressive *Steinway Mansion* sits and view it from the outside, as it awaits its next identity.

The Q101 bus stops along 20th Avenue, a block and a half away from the *Steinway Mansion* at 18-33 41st Street. You can hop on the Q101 just outside the Steinway Street subway station of the M and R trains.

Walking Distance: Steinway Piano Factory; Steinway Street (shopping).

Studio Museum in Harlem

http://www.studiomuseum.org

A neighborhood staple for five decades, the *Studio Museum in Harlem* continues to offer up the broadest array of African art and sculpture in *The City.* Of all the ethnically-themed venues in New York City (Italian American Museum, Jewish Museum, Irish Repertory Theatre), the *Studio Museum* may well have the greatest feel for the works of those that they represent.

The *Studio Museum in Harlem* was founded in 1968 and was originally located in a rented loft at 2033 Fifth Avenue, just north of 125th Street. The museum moved to 144 West 125th Street in 1979, a site donated by the New York Bank for Savings. Originally a two-level exhibition space, it has seen a number of renovations over the years. Included in those renovations was the 1985 incorporating of an adjacent lot at number 142 West 125th Street, which allowed for additional gallery and lobby space. There is also a theater and an outdoor area which can be utilized for various events. The *Artists-in-Residence* program, one of the earliest initiatives in the museum's history, is what gives the site its "*Studio*" identity. There is a constant turnover of diverse exhibits on display from the museum's collection, with a main floor and connected balcony and basement areas allowing the curators to spread the exhibits out in an organized way. The *Studio Museum* is a particularly moving venue.

Internationally known for its promotion of artistic works of those of African descent, the *Studio Museum of Harlem* connects the general public to the African community, through numerous educational and interactive programs. The *Studio Museum's* permanent collection includes nearly two thousand paintings, sculptures, watercolors, drawings, pastels, prints, photographs, mixed-media works and installations dating from the nineteenth century to the present. The massive archive of Harlem Renaissance photographer James Van Der

Zee, best known for his portraits of black New Yorkers, is part of the museum's collection.

The wide variety of programs that are offered at and by the *Studio Museum in Harlem* successfully bring art alive for enthusiasts of all ages, from very young children to the elderly. There are talks and tours available, as well as artistic activities, including performances and on- and off-site educational programs. These all contribute vibrantly to the *Studio Museum's* work. In addition, they publish their own "*Studio*" magazine twice a year and their annual export of books, exhibition catalogues and brochures are a constant reminder of how the *Studio Museum* serves the African art community.

The *Studio Museum in Harlem* is within walking distance of the 125th Street stations on the A, B, C, D, 1, 2 or 3 trains. The M2, M7, M10, M100, M101, M102 and BX 15 buses all stop nearby.

Walking Distance: Apollo Theatre; 125th Street Business Improvement District; The National Jazz Museum in Harlem; Schomburg Center

Swedish Cottage Marionette Theatre

http://www.cityparksfoundation.org/arts/swedish-cottage-marionette-theatre

The most unique of all the venues in the *Historic House Trust of New York City,* the *Swedish Cottage Marionette Theatre* is one of the best places in *The City* to bring very young children. Located just inside the 79th Street entrance of Central Park West, the *Swedish Cottage* puts on old fashioned puppet shows, using detailed marionettes to tell various classic children's tales.

For its pavilion in the 1876 Centennial Exposition in Philadelphia, Sweden built a model schoolhouse out of pine and cedar, dismantled it and re-built it upon arrival in Philadelphia. The structure was furnished with desks and chalkboards and was staffed by Swedish teachers. The Swedish pavilion was one of the most popular in the Centennial Exposition and it caught the eye of Frederick Law Olmsted, one of the designers of Central Park, who managed to get the City of New York to purchase it. The schoolhouse was dismantled again in 1877 and reconstructed on the west side of Central Park.

In 1947, eight years after the formation of a touring marionette theatre was created by the New York City Parks Commissioner, the troupe moved into the *Swedish School House*, which served as a workshop and its headquarters. In 1973, the interior of the building was redesigned to incorporate a small theater for indoor marionette performances, as well as space for the traveling theater. The *Swedish School House* thus became the *Swedish Cottage Marionette Theatre*. In 1996, the building was restored, but it still retains much of its original 19th-Century materials, including the patterned shingles and hand-rubbed interior paneling. Since then, audiences have regularly attended the *Swedish Cottage Marionette Theatre's* performances of many classic children's tales. Each production features handmade marionettes, created by masters of the craft, which contribute to the archive of historic marionettes that are collected on a yearly basis.

The City Parks Foundation, which runs the *Swedish Cottage Marionette Theatre*, also incorporates the *Puppet Mobile,* a traveling puppet show that holds performances of *Marionette Theatre* shows in parks, playgrounds and recreation centers, all around the five boroughs. As a bonus, puppet making workshops are offered where children learn about the art of puppetry and create their own puppets. The true beauty of the *Swedish Cottage Marionette Theatre* is in the setting of the cottage inside Central Park, which gives the ancient structure an almost storybook look, one that prepares children and adults for the show they're about to see.

The B or C trains to the *81st Street – Museum of Natural History* station leave you a few blocks from the 79th Street entrance to Central Park, directly across from the American Museum of Natural History. The M10 bus also stops near the park's entrance.

Walking Distance: Beacon Theatre; The Triad; Strawberry Fields; American Museum of Natural History.

The Frick Collection

http://www.frick.org

When Pittsburgh industrialist Henry Clay Frick (1848-1919), one of the world's most prominent art collectors, fled the Steel City for New York City in 1901, he envisioned a mansion which could be turned into an art museum of great substance after he had passed on. In 1906, he purchased the Lenox Library building on 5th Avenue, between 70th and 71st Streets. Frick could not take control of the land right away though, due to restrictions which had been placed on the Lenox Library site. When the Lenox collections were incorporated into the new Public Library on 42nd Street and 5th Avenue, he finally began construction on what would indeed become one of the premier art museums in not only New York, but also the United States and the world. Built in 1913-14 by the firm of Carrere and Hastings, Frick's mansion only served as his home for about five years. Upon his death in 1919, Frick left all the art and the furnishings in the house to the proposed *Frick Collection*, along with a $15 million endowment to be used for the maintenance of said collection. His wife Adelaide lived at the house until her death in 1931 and their daughter, Helen Clay Frick, ultimately oversaw the opening of *The Frick Collection* in 1935. She used the endowment to add to the museum's collections for years to come.

Helen Clay Frick (1888-1984), an art aficionado from a very young age, focused her efforts on *The Frick Collection* upon her father's death. Along with her mother and brother, Childs Frick, Helen served as a founding trustee and was the one most responsible for the early acquisitions which would enhance the collection that her father had bequeathed to the museum which had once been his lavish home. In 1920, she had also founded the *Frick Art Reference Library*, located adjacent to the museum, as a memorial to her father and as a public resource to those with an interest in art history.

The Frick Collection today consists of works in 19 galleries and a Garden Court, which is the only area where the public is allowed to take photos. A short film chronicling the history of the building plays every ½ hour, with other shorts concerning current traveling exhibits also in the mix. There are lectures, symposiums and a celebrated concert series held at the *Frick* each year. *The Frick Collection,* a remarkable personal collection, has been a New York staple for eight decades.

The 6 train to the 68th Street/Hunter College station leaves you just a few blocks from *The Frick Collection.* The M1, M2, M3 and M4 buses on 5th Avenue leave you right by *The Frick.*

Walking Distance: Central Park Zoo; Roosevelt House; Park Avenue Armory; Asia Society & Museum; The Met Breuer; The Metropolitan Museum of Art.

The Met Breuer

http://www.metmuseum.org/visit/met-breuer

The Metropolitan Museum of Art on 5th Avenue and East 82nd Street is a world famous facility and *The Met Cloisters*, located in an old monastery in the Northern most part of Fort Tryon Park in the Upper West side is one of the most amazing venues in *The City*. But there is also a much newer third site that lives under *The Met* banner. *The Met Breuer*, at 495 Madison Avenue on 75th Street, is a short walk from the main branch and serves well as a complimentary building to the much larger galleries of the original.

The Met Breuer (pronounced Broy-er) opened on March 18, 2016 in the former home of the *Whitney Museum of Art*. When the Whitney moved to a new facility in the Meatpacking District, its former space eventually became available. The moniker *The Met Breuer* was adopted by using the name of the architect of the building, Hungarian born Marcel Breuer (1902–1981), who received the commission to build a new museum of American art in New York in 1963, after becoming famous for his mastery of stone and concrete with institutional buildings and private homes across Europe. That building became *The Whitney*. The sale made, the lobby was renovated for the opening of *The Met Breuer* and *The Met* leased the building from the Whitney group.

The Met Breuer offers the public the art of the 20th and 21st centuries. There are a large range of exhibitions, commissions, performances, and artist residencies that are now born out of this site. As *The Met's* main branch is well known for its wide-ranging collection of ancient art, *The Met Breuer* was opened with the idea of using it to showcase contemporary art, which had become more widespread in the New York art community in the past few decades. There are four floors of spacious exhibition galleries, which *The*

Whitney had become famous for and thus passed on to the newest member of *The Met* family.

One of the unique things about *The Met* properties is that a visitor can use his or her admission for any one of the sites to access either of the other two on the same day, which is most reasonable in regard to *The Met Breuer* and the main branch, which are only a few blocks apart. Visiting *The Met Cloisters* on the west side and way uptown is a bit more of a chore for one day, though.

The 6 train to the 77th Street station leaves you just a few blocks from *The Met Breuer*. The M1, M2, M3 and M4 buses on Madison Avenue (uptown) and 5th Avenue (downtown) all stop within short walking distance.

<u>Walking Distance</u>: The Frick Collection; The Metropolitan Museum of Art; Asia Society & Museum; Park Avenue Armory; Roosevelt House; The Meatball Shop.

The Met Cloisters at Fort Tryon Park

http://www.metmuseum.org/visit/met-cloisters

The perfect merging of artifacts and location in New York City can be found at *The Met Cloisters* in Fort Tryon Park, near the northern tip of Manhattan. This majestic branch of *The Metropolitan Museum of Art* is not only unique to anything one can find in *The City*, it is also timeless, which adds to the venue's mystique.

Philanthropist John D. Rockefeller was the driving force behind the creation of *The Cloisters*, beginning in 1917, when he commissioned the development of the site. As part of the project, Rockefeller purchased the medieval art collection of George Grey Barnard, an American sculptor and collector, and pooled it with holdings of his own, including the *Unicorn Tapestries*, a set of seven tapestries, made between 1495 and 1505, which now occupy their own room inside *The Met Cloisters*. Barnard and Rockefeller's collection formed the foundation for *The Cloisters*.

The building gets its name from the architectural elements and settings relocated from four French medieval abbeys. The Cuxa, Bonnefort, Trie and Saint-Guilhem cloisters were transported, reconstructed and integrated within the new building by architect Charles Collens, between 1934 and 1939. Amongst these cloisters, the museum presents more than 2,000 exceptional artworks and architectural elements from the Medieval West.

Walking through *The Met Cloisters* today, it's very easy to propel yourself back some 600 years, to the 15th Century times that the works on this site originate from. The gardens, chapels and halls that integrate with the relocated French cloisters help form an almost breathing mosaic of an ancient monastery. The sculptures found throughout the grounds are impressive beyond category. Even the huge arched doorways and the heavy wooden door that leads to the

West Terrace, a veranda that offers a spectacular view of the Hudson River and the George Washington Bridge, are evocative in their own way. *The Met Cloisters* is another must see New York site. Naturally, being a part of *The Metropolitan Museum of Art* family means that all the educational programs and special events offered by *The Met* extend to the patrons of *The Met Cloisters.* Above all, experiencing all of the impressive art and sculpture at *The Met Cloisters*, in the realm of such spectacular architecture, creates a mood unlike any that one can find in New York City.

If you take the A train to 190th Street and go up the elevator at the north end of the station, you will be right outside Fort Tryon Park. From there, you walk inside the park, through Margaret Corbin Drive, for about 10 minutes, following the signs to *The Met Cloisters.* You can also take the M4 bus North, one stop from the park entrance, to *The Cloisters.*

Walking Distance: Hudson River; George Washington Bridge; Inwood Hill Park; Dyckman Farmhouse Museum; Good Shepherd Church.

The Museum of the American Gangster

http://siteline2.vendini.com/site/museumoftheamericangangster.org

People who live in a city as populated as New York know that crime most certainly exists, whether they have been a victim or not. A most pointed and unrivaled museum in New York that looks into the underworld element is the *Museum of the American Gangster*, located at 78-80 St. Mark's Place in the East Village.

The *Museum of the American Gangster* takes a hands-on approach to their subject matter, with an involved, detailed, guided tour at the centerpiece of its presentation. Not one, but two tour guides alternately bring visitors from the rollicking days of Prohibition into the current, much quieter times of the understated mob. The museum consists of a pair of rooms lined with photos and artifacts that the guides use to illustrate the tale of crime in not just New York City, but across the country. And as the museum is located on the site of a former speakeasy, each tour finishes with a trek to what once housed the underground tunnels beneath the speakeasy.

Famous gangland figures like Meyer Lansky and Bugsy Siegel are among the prints on a wall that celebrates the Jewish faction of what would become organized crime. Infamous gambling czar Arnold Rothstein, the man who fixed the 1919 World Series, is also prominent. Newspaper reproductions chronicle the St. Valentine's Day Massacre and photos of Al Capone, Dion O'Bannion and Bugs Moran also help recall the violent days of 1920's gangland Chicago. Topics range from how to make bootleg gin, the questions surrounding the death of John Dillinger and the mythical nature of FBI crime boss J. Edgar Hoover, who is refreshingly portrayed as maybe the most corrupt of all those pictured on the walls. A painting by and a suit once owned by contemporary mobster Henry Hill are other resident artifacts.

The descent into the old tunnels of the Scheib speakeasy, which once occupied 78-80 St. Mark's Place, provides a great capper to the stories told in the *Museum of the American Gangster.* To get down there, you go through a working bar and the Theatre 80, an off-Broadway stage that still operates where there once was an escape tunnel. The tunnels themselves are modest, but do contain an old safe and a pair of ancient telephones that the mobsters used to receive alerts from upstairs. The *Museum of the American Gangster* is a most curious *City* museum.

The 6 train to Astor Place leaves you a few blocks from the *Museum of the American Gangster* at 78-80 St. Mark's Place. The R and N trains to 8th Street and Broadway are two blocks further away, but within easy walking distance.

Walking Distance: Tompkins Square Park; S'Mac; New Museum; Basilica at Old St. Patrick's Cathedral; The Meatball Shop.

Ukrainian Museum

http://www.ukrainianmuseum.org

Of the many ethnically centered museums in *The City*, one of the most polished is the *Ukrainian Museum*, located in the East Village, at 222 East 6th Street, between Second and Third Avenues. The *Ukrainian Museum*, is, in fact, the largest museum committed to acquiring, preserving, exhibiting and interpreting articles of historic significance from the Ukrainian people. It was founded in 1976 by the *Ukrainian National Women's League of America* and was instantly hailed as one of the most significant achievements in the Ukrainian American community. Today, the *Ukrainian Museum*, with its large collection of folk art and an ever growing archival cache, is a venue with a much broader appeal than just to natives or descendants of the Ukraine.

The current home of the *Ukrainian Museum*, a building designed by Ukrainian American architect George Zawicki, opened in 2005, with large galleries on two floors and a basement level. The museum's collections are broken down into three categories:

1.) The Folk Art Collection – contains over 8,000 objects, including ritual cloths, wedding and other festive attire and embroidered and woven textiles. Ceramics, metalwork and wood carved objects are also part of this collection, as is an impressive collection of *pysanky*, or Ukrainian Easter eggs.
2.) The Fine Art Collection – contains over 2,000 paintings, sculptures, drawings and graphic works by noted Ukrainians who worked in the Ukraine, Europe and the United States, predominantly in the 20th Century.
3.) The Archives – more than 30,000 items are housed in the museum's archives, which chart (among other things) the history of Ukrainian immigration to the United States. The archives also contain a collection of 17th and 18th Century

maps, some 16th century coins and currency from the early 20th Century to the present.

I found the *Ukrainian Museum* to be most fascinating, with many rich oil paintings and disparate sculptures the most alluring to me. A 1924 painting called "Harlem River" by David Burliuk (1882-1967) and a pair of wire sculptures by Konstantin Milonadis (1926-2012) were particularly appealing.

There are a wide range of public programs at the *Ukrainian Museum* each year, including lectures, conferences, gallery talks, symposiums and book presentations. A program of documentary and feature films has also recently been implemented. Books, jewelry, CDs, DVDs and a variety of *pysanky* are available in the first floor gift shop.

The N or R trains to 8th Street leave you a few blocks from the *Ukrainian Museum*, as does the 6 train to Astor Place and the F train to 2nd Avenue. The M101, M102 and M103 buses have Third Avenue stops by the museum and the M15 on Second Avenue (southbound) and First Avenue (northbound) also leave you a short walk from the museum.

Walking Distance: Merchant's House Museum; Washington Square Park; Triangle Shirtwaist Factory site; New Museum; The Basilica at Old St. Patrick's Cathedral; Tompkins Square Park; The Meatball Shop.

Valentine-Varian House (Bronx Historical Society Museum)

http://bronxhistoricalsociety.org

The last farmhouse standing in The Bronx of those that once made up the Boston Post Road, the *Valentine-Varian House* serves as the home of the *Bronx Historical Society Museum*. Now located inside Williamsbridge Oval Park at 208th Street and Bainbridge Avenue, the *Valentine-Varian House*, named after the first two families that owned the property, dates back to before the Revolutionary War.

The house was built in 1758 by Isaac Valentine, a farmer and blacksmith from Yonkers, who used the stones on his property to construct this home. The location gave Valentine a lot of business as a blacksmith, with carts and carriages constantly passing on the way to King's Bridge and Manhattan. It also gave him good access to New York's crop markets. Things went south for Valentine during the Revolutionary War, though, when the British and Colonial armies alternately controlled the area in and around the bridge. The family remained on the property for the most part, though they did abandon the home for an 11-month period in 1775-1776. Valentine eventually went into deep debt and lost the house in the late 18th Century.

Isaac Varian, a farmer and butcher, bought the house and 260-acre farm from the struggling Valentine in 1792. Three generations of Varians would own the home. When Isaac died in 1820, his son, Michael, assumed control. Michael Varian's son Jesse would succeed his father as homeowner and farmer. As the area grew rapidly in the dawn of the 20th Century, farming the land became much harder and Jesse Varian sold it to a developer. In 1905, William F. Beller bought the house at auction, along with what by then was a much smaller piece of land. The Beller family remained on site until 1965, when Beller's son, William C. Beller, donated the house to the Bronx

County Historical Society. It was then that the house was moved from its original site to the current location in Williamsbridge Oval Park. The *Valentine-Varian House* opened to the public as the *Museum of Bronx History* in 1968.

Today, there are three rooms which offer exhibits that collectively form the *Bronx Historical Society Museum.* A permanent timeline of the area and the house is in the front parlor and rotating exhibits are presented in the two facing rooms. There is a small gift shop in the rear of the house and there are various public and school programs offered at the *Valentine-Varian House.*

The final stop on the D train, Norwood/205th Street & Bainbridge Avenue leaves you just a few blocks from the *Valentine-Varian House* and the *Bronx Historical Society Museum.* The Bx10, Bx16, Bx28, Bx30, Bx34 and Bx38 buses stop right by the museum.

Walking Distance: Williamsbridge Oval Park; Montefiore Medical Center.

Van Cortlandt House Museum

http://www.vchm.org

In a building that was once utilized by both British and Colonial military factions during the Revolutionary War, the *Van Cortlandt House Museum* is yet another of the great preserved mansions in New York City. Located inside the vast *Van Cortlandt Park* in The Bronx, this structure still maintains a great aura and is definitely a site that City dwellers should consider visiting.

The oldest building in The Bronx today, it was constructed by Frederick Van Cortlandt in 1748, as the headquarters for a grain plantation and grist mill that was built around the property. The Van Cortlandts were a prominent New York family who ran a successful wheat plantation. The *Van Cortlandt House* was occupied by the family and its slaves until 1889, when the surrounding property was sold to the City of New York and made into a public park. The National Society of Colonial Dames in the State of New York, who specialize in preserving our national heritage through historic preservation and educational projects, took on the *Van Cortlandt House* in 1896 and began operating the house as a public museum in 1897, making it New York City's first historic house museum. Added to the National Register of Historic Places in 1967, the *Van Cortlandt House Museum* was named a National Historic Landmark in 1976.

Much like the *Merchant's House* in Manhattan, the *Van Cortlandt House Museum* offers a self-guided tour, with a small folder describing the rooms and grounds given upon admission. The three floors of the house feature period piece furniture and accoutrements, to give the feel of life in the times of an 18th century New York family. The East and West Parlors on the first floor show how guests were accommodated in the daytime and feature a style that represents the Van Cortlandts' Dutch lineage. Three chambers on the second floor, of various sizes, reflect a pecking order. The West Chamber, believed to be used by George Washington in the days he stayed at the *Van Cortlandt House*, was a slightly more preferred room than the East Chamber. The Dutch Chamber, which is accessed by going through the East Chamber, provided eating and sleeping quarters for small families. The third floor consists of a Nursery Room and the so-called Unfinished Chamber, which was used mostly as a storage area or as sleeping grounds for enslaved workers. An herb garden in front of the house was essential for the meals that the family and guests ate.

The final stop on the 1 train, 242nd Street, leaves you adjacent to *Van Cortlandt Park*, with the *Van Cortlandt House Museum* 4 blocks up, at 246th Street. The Bx9 bus stops on 244th street.

Walking Distance: Van Cortlandt Park

Final Destination

Brooklyn Heights Promenade

https://www.nycgovparks.org/about/history/historical-signs/listings?id=136

Sightseeing is a main attraction, whether you are coming to or living in New York City. Naturally, there are certain spots where the sights are most vibrant. One of these is the *Brooklyn Heights Promenade*, a small, vertical park that overlooks a number of New York City landmarks.

In the Civil War Era, Brooklyn Heights consisted of mostly private gardens, right near the shore, that looked out toward Manhattan, Liberty and Ellis Islands. Wealthy residents were said to "*promenade*" along the waterfront, which later gave the area that name. A quote, attributed to President Abraham Lincoln in 1864 (from the Parks Department website) states "*There may be finer views than this in the world, but I don't believe it.*" Hezekiah Pierrepont, a wealthy resident of Brooklyn Heights, had first proposed a promenade area in 1827, for the elite of Brooklyn to enjoy. Pierrepont's vision didn't come to fruition for over a century and when it did, the *Brooklyn Heights Promenade* would be utilized not just by the rich people, but by New Yorkers of all stripes.

In 1941, the New York City Planning Commission under Robert Moses wanted to run the Brooklyn-Queens Expressway right through Brooklyn Heights, but they were fought off successfully by the neighborhood. A few years later, a second proposal produced a suggestion by a resident for a double-decked highway, ostensibly to save his personal gardens. This resultant "cover" for the highway (Interstate 278) below would be the *Brooklyn Heights Promenade*, which was dedicated on October 7, 1950. From the very beginning, this 1,826 foot pedestrian walkway, complete with park benches at its fore, became arguably the best lookout point in *The City.*

These days, from the rails at the *Brooklyn Heights Promenade*, the views to the right, of the Brooklyn Bridge and Downtown Manhattan, featuring South Street Seaport and the new Freedom Tower, are breathtaking. To the left, the perspectives on the Statue of Liberty, Ellis Island and Governor's Island are most unique. Many local residents, or those who work in the area, can often be seen eating their lunches, while relaxing on a Promenade bench. New mothers pushing their children in carriages or strollers are another regular sight. There are a few commemorative plaques in the small park. One is for local civic leader Genevieve Beavers Earle (1885-1956) and another is for a structure that once stood there, the "Four Chimneys" House, which served as a headquarters for General George Washington during the Battle of Long Island in 1776. The Promenade is open 24 hours.

If you take the 2, 3, 4, 5, N or R trains to the Borough Hall Station, then walk down Montague Street, you'll flow right into the *Brooklyn Heights Promenade*.

Walking Distance: Brooklyn Historical Society Museum; New York Transit Museum; Jackie Robinson Plaque; 133 Clinton Street Plaque; Metrotech Business Improvement District; Fulton Mall; Brooklyn War Memorial.

A City Block

(Ode to Saint Jane)

As I walk through a city block,
especially in the Village main,
I recall the threat of arrogance,
as I pray to our Saint Jane.

Faces make me smile and allocute
that I love each one the same;
This no matter if they looked like me,
or even if they knew my name.

In the quiet manic of a city block
you can feel ancestors calling;
We can live as one among millions,
with our neighborhoods not falling.

You know, the old fool never drove a car,
yet thought highways were an answer;
Till the folks on Broome Street spoke up
for every dedicated street romancer.

Should you see me on a city block,
toss a nod and walk on by;
Just remember, we are ours together,
should you pause to stop and sigh.

I have walked from Mulberry to the Heights;
From the east to the west side grand;
And I chuckle at that unseen traffic jam
that that people hater planned.

Much as I revere my family roots,
I am thrilled by other kinds;
And Saint Jane still walks on a city block
in our hearts and souls and minds.

About The Author

Thomas Porky McDonald is the author of 22 previous books, including 9 poetry collections, a book of short stories and A Walk in the City, An Incomplete Tour, an earlier volume of New York City travel destinations.